EXTRAORDINARY RECIPES FROM

DENVER & BOULDER CHEF'S TABLE

RUTH TOBIAS

Photography by Christopher Cina

THE COLORADO FRONT RANGE

LYONS PRESS
Guilford, Connecticut

An imprint of Globe Pequot Press

Lyons Press is an imprint of Globe Pequot Press.

All photography by Christopher Cina

Editor: Kevin Sirois
Project Editor: Tracee Williams
Text Design: Libby Kingsbury
Layout Artist: Nancy Freeborn

Library of Congress Cataloging-in-Publication Data

Tobias, Ruth, 1970-
  Denver & Boulder chef's table : extraordinary recipes from the Colorado Front Range / Ruth Tobias ; photography by Christopher Cina. — First [edition].
    pages cm
  Summary: "Landscape has everything to do with who Coloradans are and thus how they cook, eat, and drink. With a spotlight on cooking traditions from around the world, the Front Range dining scene has never felt so exciting and vibrant, all the while set against a singular backdrop: the Rocky Mountains. *Denver & Boulder Chef's Table* gathers the cities' best chefs and restaurants under one roof, featuring recipes for the home cook from over fifty of the region's most celebrated restaurants and showcasing full-color photos of mouth-watering dishes, award-winning chefs, and lots of local flavor"— Provided by publisher.
  ISBN 978-0-7627-8640-4 (hardback)
  1. Cooking, American—Western style. 2. Cooking—Colorado—Denver. 3. Cooking—Colorado—Boulder. 4. Restaurants—Colorado—Denver—Guidebooks. 5. Restaurants—Colorado—Boulder—Guidebooks. 6. Denver (Colo.)—Guidebooks. 7. Boulder (Colo.)—Guidebooks. I. Title. II. Title: Denver and Boulder chef's table.
  TX715.2.W47T63 2013
  641.59788—dc23

                                                                                              2013017845

Printed in the United States of America

10 9 8 7 6 5 4 3 2 1

Restaurants and chefs often come and go, and menus are ever-changing.
We recommend you call ahead to obtain current information before
visiting any of the establishments in this book.

CONTENTS

HOUSE MADE FRIES

CHARRED TAHINI CAULIFLOWER
FULL ORDERS ONLY

MIXED GREEN SALAD

DESSERT OF THE DAY $3⁹⁵

ICE-CREAM SANDWICHES
$3⁹⁵

DEEP FRIED MAC N CHEESE

FRIED GREEN TOMATOES

SIDE SALAD

HAND CUT POTATO CHIPS

BIKER BAKED BEANS

ASK ABOUT OUR SPECIALS

BIKER JIM'S CLASSIC
CREAM CHEESE & CARAMELIZED ONION

THE CONEY
RICH MEATY NOT TOO SPICY NEW JERSEY STYLE CHILI
WITH DICED ONION AND YELLOW MUSTARD

THE DESERT
HARISSA ROASTED CACTUS
MALAYSIAN JAM SCALLIONS CILANTRO & ONIONS 2 WAYS

THE SONORAN
PINTOS JALAPENOS TOMATOES
ONIONS, YELLOW MUSTARD & MAYO

THE INTERNATIONAL
WASABI AIOLI CARAMELIZED APPLE
SHAVED IRISH CHEDDAR

ELK J
That pretty much sums u

WILD
Apricots & cranberries co

We sincerely apologize
wrangler was in a tr
wrangling accident so w
out of stock on our rat
dog. We hope to have
apologize for the i

GERMAN
Very Traditional, Very G

LING
Portuguese style pork sa

ALL
The perfect all America

NOT TO BE

BAT DO
SMOKED BACON
AVOCADO PU
TOMATO CREAM CH
CARAMELIZED ONION, BACC

$7⁵⁰

ASK ABO

Acknowledgments

I didn't write this cookbook: The restaurateurs and chefs who contributed recipes did. They are scholars and gentlefolk, and it goes without saying that they deserve my utmost gratitude. Editing their recipes was an exercise in inspiration.

I didn't take the photographs for this cookbook: Christopher Cina, himself a professional chef, did that, visiting some locations two and three times to ensure he got the perfect shot—all while becoming a father for the third time. Cina was a down-to-earth delight to work with, as was our editor at Globe Pequot, Kevin Sirois. (Of course, I already knew that, having collaborated with him on the 2012 edition of the *Food Lovers' Guide to Denver & Boulder.*)

What I did do, above all, was coordinate, coordinate, coordinate—aided in the process by a squadron of behind-the-scenes players. Huge thanks go, in alphabetical order, to Kuvy Ax, Jordan Beyer, Kristen Browning-Blas, Douglas Brown, Bryce Clark, Aubrey Cornelius, Ashley Cothran, Amanda Faison, Lauren Hendrick, T. J. Hobbs, John Imbergamo, Stefanie Jones, Nina Kocher, Kate Lacroix, John Lehndorff, Dara Levine, Adrian Miller, Cristin Napier, Brenda Orozco, Lauren Feder Place, Dev Ranjan, Nikki Schaeffer, Emily Schwartz, Lu Stasko, Leigh Sullivan, Cassidy Tawse, Sylvia Tawse, Jennifer Walker, and Danny Wang.

What I also did, undoubtedly, was try the patience of my loved ones over the course of this months-long project. Granted, since my parents, Henry and Haven Tobias, raised me to value diligence, I trust they ultimately empathize. As for Brit Withey—I couldn't have done it, or much else, without his support. He's a keeper.

Introduction

In the summer of 2011, I began work on *Food Lovers' Guide to Denver & Boulder* (Globe Pequot Press) with the confidence of a freelance writer/blogger who had already logged countless hours exploring the local dining scene: I had a lot to say but not, I thought, a lot left to learn about the restaurants and bars and markets around me.

The research experience was thus a humbling one. According to the estimate of local alt weekly *Westword,* some three hundred new eateries opened that year—nearly one a day; keeping up proved a Sisyphean enterprise, as I scouted out this or that hot spot in LoDo (Lower Downtown), the Highlands to the north, City and Congress Parks as well as Cherry Creek to the west, and the Baker District, Washington Park, and Old South Pearl to the south. Scattered among them were countless mom-and-pop operations of all ethnic stripes, surviving on hyperlocal word of mouth; to find them, I had to cover every last stretch of pavement from Arvada to Aurora and Littleton to the north Boulder outskirts. In short, I wound up learning a great deal—and fast—about just how diverse and dynamic the Front Range community really is.

Of course, by the time the *Food Lovers' Guide* hit bookshelves in mid-2012, some of my favorite discoveries had closed, soon-to-be favorites were arriving left and right— and I had been offered the opportunity to pen the book you're holding now. It seemed a golden one insofar as I could try to capture herein not just what the culinary artisans of Denver and Boulder do so well but how they do it, how they think. Names and locations change; the creative process per se does not. Recipes are forever.

Which doesn't mean they don't speak to a specific time and place. Certain ingredients and techniques have their moments in Colorado's near-constant sun; long-lost customs are revived and new ones forged. Consider, for instance, the two extremes of the homesteading movement and the rise of molecular gastronomy (to use an admittedly controversial but nonetheless recognizable term). On the one hand are chefs turned farmers, dairymen, and ranchers—growing their own crops, making their own cheese, even raising their own livestock; on the other, you've got mad scientists concocting comestibles out of thin air almost literally, with the help of immersion circulators and nitrogen dispensers and smoking guns. Or take the ever-shifting yet ever–more precisely trained spotlight on cooking traditions around the world: Today we speak less of, say, Chinese cuisine than we do of Sichuan or Fujian, less of Mexican than Pueblan or Michoacán, and our pantries are lined with products from Morocco, Indonesia, and the South Tyrol. Tomorrow, for all we know, the focus may be on Panama and Kazakhstan. Meanwhile, these trends take shape, these influences reveal themselves, against a singular backdrop: the Rocky Mountains.

Landscape has everything to do with who Coloradans are and thus how they cook, eat, and drink. Ruggedness is a given: The cowboys and outlaws of the old Wild West have their modern-day equivalents in extreme athletes and back-to-the-land enthusiasts who forage for forest mushrooms when they're not tending to their beehives and chicken coops. Sanguinity and a sense of adventure are its corollaries—traits that

equip a young and healthy population to thrive in a high, dry, sometimes harsh climate that, while not ideal for all living things, certainly also yields extraordinary buffalo and lamb and freshwater fish as well as bumper sweet corn, peaches, and melons. And of course, where there's a penchant for working hard and playing hard, there's an appetite for booze. Our vineyards may struggle—though pioneering winemakers are working to change that, with some hard-won success—but our world-class craft-beer industry has inspired a growing number of hops and barley farmers as well as a parallel boom in microdistilleries.

These local, seasonal products are featured in our kitchens every day, and this book celebrates them as well as the chefs and bartenders who put them to good use. Some recipes require only basic skills and equipment; others call for rather more experience and gadgetry galore, not to mention discipline with respect to *mise en place,* to use the kitchen term for advance preparation. Either way, we encourage you to do as Coloradans do: Take the plunge, experiment—and above all, have loads of fun.

MILE-HIGH CITY ON THE RISE

As longtime food editor at *5280,* Amanda Faison has seen Colorado cuisine grow from seed to full blossom. We asked her to describe its evolution over the course of her tenure at the magazine: How does she view it today, and what aspects excite her most?

I've been at *5280* for sixteen years—which is long enough, I think, to gain some perspective on our dining scene. Early on, we at the magazine talked a lot about local restaurants' identity crisis: With the exception of steak houses, they rarely seemed comfortable being true to their roots. I think that was due to the influx of transplants from influential cities such as New York or San Francisco, who wanted Denver to be more like the places they had left. It was my sense that local chefs didn't know what to think—and they often spent more time trying to please the newcomers than representing Colorado as a whole.

Although Denver remains a melting pot, I see a huge change in chef confidence. We aren't New York or San Francisco, and we don't want to be: We are Denver. That means we watch our growing cycles shift in and out of drought. It means making pie with sun-ripened Palisade peaches, grilling buttery Olathe corn, and dousing whatever we can find in fiery green chile. It means sourcing quinoa from the San Luis Valley, eating sweet and tender Colorado lamb, and turning our crisp mountain water into award-winning craft beers. It means raising bees on top of the historic Brown Palace downtown (see Palace Arms, page 132) and nurturing projects like the Grow Haus, an urban farm amid a sea of asphalt. It means having pride in our state, honoring our lifestyle (show me a restaurant in which you can't wear jeans), and celebrating who we are.

Ace Eat Serve

501 East 17th Avenue
Denver, CO 80203
(303) 800-7705
acedenver.com
Owners: Josh and Jenny Wolkon
Chef: Brandon Biederman

Retro, eclectic, electric: Ace Eat Serve runs on sheer verve. Uproariously decked out in the repurposed flotsam and jetsam of the garage that preceded it, along with vintage kitsch from Thailand and a phalanx of Ping Pong tables, this Uptown hang was built for the cool kids by the cool kids, namely co-owner Josh Wolkon, executive chef Brandon Biederman, and longtime toque Matt Selby (who's now running his own place, Corner House). Leave it to the masterminds behind the ever-sizzling Steuben's (page 173), next door to Ace, and LoDo's Vesta Dipping Grill (page 196) to tack a rec room onto a pan-Asian snack bar, freewheeling cocktail lounge, and patio—and somehow make it all work as smoothly as the jalopies that used to roll out of here.

Of course, the anything-goes vibe is a bit deceptive; the open secret to these guys' success is, after all, that they're sticklers for detail. Heck, the killer condiments practically make for a meal in themselves, from the jars of fermented black beans and sesame-seed paste atop every table to the mustard-seed relish accompanying the funky-fresh *bao* (try the one stuffed with chicken thigh and pickled mango). Proper sticky rice comes nestled in a cute little bamboo basket. Locally churned ice cream fills delicate pastel *mochi*. And the mixologists don't miss a trick—spiking zingy house-made sodas with phosphate, snow cones with *soju,* and a brain-scrambling array of tropical concoctions with the likes of ice coffee, oolong-tea syrup, and chili sugar.

By the same token, table tennis isn't a free-for-all—the sharp-eyed staff enforces such house rules as "Rackets may only hit balls, not people" and "Absolutely NO beer pong." But as for the ultimate commandment—"Have fun!"—that hardly needs spelling out. At Ace, you couldn't possibly do otherwise.

Crispy Beef with Spicy Sauce

Sambal oelek is an Indonesian chili paste that, along with a few other ingredients in this recipe, should be available at any Asian grocery. Chef Brandon Biederman recommends serving this dish over steamed rice or Asian-style noodles, such as *chow fun.*

(SERVES 4)

For the sauce:

¾ cup light soy sauce

4 tablespoons honey

3 tablespoons rice wine vinegar

2 tablespoons cooking rice wine

4 tablespoons turbinado sugar

1½ tablespoons *sambal oelek*

2 ounces ginger, peeled and julienned

3 tablespoons cornstarch

½ cup water

For the beef:

8 cups peanut oil

4 cups cornstarch

2 tablespoons salt

2 tablespoons freshly ground black pepper

2 pounds flank steak, sliced thin on the bias
against the grain

2 tablespoons sesame oil

4 tablespoons julienned fresh ginger

2 tablespoons minced garlic

1 tablespoon minced bird (Thai) chili

1 tablespoon minced lemongrass, white part
of stalk only

2 Kaffir lime leaves, whole

Special equipment:

frying thermometer

wok

To make the sauce: In a nonreactive sauce pot over low heat, bring all sauce ingredients except cornstarch and water to a simmer. Combine cornstarch and water in a mixing bowl to make a slurry. Once the pot is simmering, add the slurry; return the mixture to a simmer, whisking continuously until it thickens, then lower heat to keep warm.

To make the beef: In a large pot over medium heat, bring peanut oil to 350°F. Meanwhile, combine the cornstarch, salt, and pepper in a bowl and dredge the steak slices in the mixture, shaking off any excess. Fry the meat in batches (so as not to overcrowd the pot) until crispy, about 2 minutes per batch.

Add sesame oil to a wok or sauté pan over high heat; when hot, add remaining ingredients and sauté until fragrant. Measure in 1–1½ cups of the reserved sauce, bring to a boil, and reduce until slightly thickened, about 1 minute. Again working in batches as necessary, add fried steak slices and toss quickly to coat. Serve immediately.

Arugula Bar e Ristorante

2785 Iris Avenue
Boulder, CO 80304
(303) 443-5100
arugularistorante.com
Chef/Owner: Alec Schuler

As crisp as its namesake green, Alec Schuler's flagship exudes Italian style against the unlikeliest of backdrops: a North Boulder strip mall. Beneath a candle-topped iron chandelier, the elegantly simple dining room gleams in creamy beige and brown-black tones; the floors are polished no less than the glassware set atop white-linen runners. And the menu follows suit, locating itself neatly between *fattoria-a-forchetta* (that is, farm-to-fork) tradition and cosmopolitanism. At the comforting end of the spectrum are Vin Santo–glazed *pâté di campagna* and white beans stewed with pancetta; on the other, ever-evolving end, you may find frothy cantaloupe soup—Prosecco-infused and pistachio-studded—or gnocchi strewn with a confetti of caramelized pears, almonds, and Gorgonzola.

Meanwhile, the wine list occupies its own sweet spot as a compendium primarily of regional finds from the Boot, as opposed to collectors' trophies— which means it's as fascinating as it is reasonable, a double whammy for oenophiles. (We're talking sparkling red Brachetto, Piedmontese Roero Arneis, Lagrein from Alto Adige . . .) Such *amore di vino* suffuses not only the dining room but the sleekly artsy adjacent lounge, Amaro Drinkery Italia, where Schuler hosts regular multicourse wine dinners in addition to offering happy-hour deals on craft cocktails and local microbrews as well as house pours.

Yet another door down, the aptly named Tangerine (2777 Iris Avenue; 303-443-2333; tangerineboulder.com) is Schuler's hat trick—a citrus-bright daytime spot where espressos and blackberry Bellinis pair as naturally with the likes of buttermilk biscuits in duck-confit gravy as Primitivo does with Arugula's orecchiette in buffalo Bolognese. Come for the toast with jelly—stay for the toast with Ribolla Gialla. *A la dolce vita!*

Pork Scaloppini with Speck
& Montasio Potatoes

Speck is a salt-cured, lightly smoked, juniper-scented ham from South Tyrol, readily available at gourmet retailers.

(SERVES 6)

2¼ pounds pork tenderloin

3 pounds fingerling, red, or new potatoes,
    cut into 1-inch cubes

Olive oil as directed

Salt and pepper to taste

10 ounces Montasio cheese (or other good-quality
    Alpine cow's milk cheese, such as swiss), sliced

Flour for dredging

3 ounces (6 tablespoons) unsalted butter, cut into
    pieces

12 large fresh sage leaves, roughly chopped

¼ cup pine nuts

½ cup beef stock

8 ounces speck ham or prosciutto crudo,
    thinly sliced

4 teaspoons fresh lemon juice

Special equipment:

meat mallet

Preheat the oven to 400°F.

Remove the silver skin from the pork and cut it into 12 medallions (about 3 ounces each). Cover with plastic wrap and pound with a mallet to approximately ¼-inch thickness.

Coat potato cubes well in olive oil and salt, place in a baking dish, and roast in the oven until tender throughout, about 25 minutes; about 2–4 minutes before they're done, lay the sliced cheese over them so it melts.

Coat the bottom of a sauté pan with olive oil (a couple of tablespoons should suffice) and place over medium-high heat. Sprinkle one side of the pork scaloppini with salt and pepper; dredge the pieces in flour and sear for 2 minutes, browning the edges. Flip the pieces over and add the butter, sage, and pine nuts. Cook another 2–3 minutes, then add the beef stock. Remove the pork immediately and allow the sauce to reduce by about one-third while you build six serving plates: Place a mound of cheesy potatoes on each, and lean two pieces of pork against each mound. Lay the sliced ham on the pork. Stir the lemon juice into the reduced sauce and pour over the top.

Sweet Potato, Parsnip & Beet Gratin

(SERVES 12 AS A SIDE DISH OR 6 AS AN ENTREE)

2 large sweet potatoes

2 large beets

3 medium parsnips

Olive oil (or butter) as directed

Salt and pepper to taste

2 tablespoons roughly chopped fresh thyme

7 ounces gruyère (or any swiss cheese), grated

5 ounces fresh goat cheese, crumbled

1½ cups heavy cream

Special equipment:

mandoline (optional)

Preheat the oven to 350°F.

Slice the sweet potatoes, beets, and parsnips lengthwise on a mandoline (or carefully with a knife) to yield pieces approximately ⅜-inch thick.

Rub a 9 x 11-inch casserole dish with a little olive oil (or butter if you prefer).

Layer the vegetables into the casserole: Start with the parsnips; sprinkle with salt, pepper, a pinch of thyme, and a portion of either of the cheeses. Repeat the process with the beets and the other cheese; then with the sweet potato and the first cheese, and so on. Be sure the top layer is sweet potato, and reserve enough gruyère to completely cover the top. Push the layers down forcefully to compact them.

Pour cream over the layers, aiming for the crevices so it seeps to the bottom. Cover first in plastic wrap and then in aluminum foil, both tightly. Bake in oven for 2 hours. Uncover and let rest 5–10 minutes before cutting and serving. This dish reheats well (covered) and freezes well, too.

Beatrice & Woodsley

38 South Broadway
Denver, CO 80209
(303) 777-3505
BEATRICEANDWOODSLEY.COM
Owners: Kevin Delk and John Skogstad; Chef: Pete List

Calling Beatrice & Woodsley a restaurant is like calling the moon a rock—technically correct but hardly revealing. At heart (to allude to its arrow-pierced logo, designed to resemble graffiti carved into tree bark with a penknife), this Baker District destination is a historical romance that unfolds in three dimensions—and envelops all who enter in its mystique.

Co-owner Kevin Delk took inspiration for the design from the nineteenth-century tale of a young woodcutter in California who fell in love with a winemaker's daughter and whisked her off to Colorado, where he built the mountain cabin for two that every nook and cranny of the earth-toned dining room re-create. Aspen trunks reach to a vaulted ceiling hung with glowing lanterns; gauzy drapes suggest wisps of fog; wall-mounted chainsaws support back-bar shelves in startling array. And in a branch-covered vestibule

leading to the restrooms, the pull of a wooden handle turns long strands of silver beads into a trickling waterfall that streams into a galvanized-tin washbasin. The effect is simply breathtaking.

And it's reinforced by a gloriously idiosyncratic seasonal menu that captures the spirit of the American frontier while cresting the wave of the future. Imagine grilled lamb-liver-and-kidney pie brightened by a dollop of currant piccalilli. Hearty cobblers of wilted greens and sausage topped with cheddar spoon bread. Airy Indian pudding *brûlée* over jalapeño-rosemary grits, and even tender yak-mincemeat pie beneath a scoop of sweet potato–toffee ice cream. Finally, supplementing the equally dreamy cocktails is a wine list steeped in intrigue, thanks to finds like a sparkling Australian Shiraz or a crisp Rkatsiteli from Macedonia. Here's to the very stuff of happy ever-afters.

Scottish Salmon Tartare with Sweet Corn Vinaigrette, Charred Haricots Verts & Herb Salad

Espelette pepper (*piment d'Espelette*) is a type of French paprika that should be available, along with Champagne vinegar, in most gourmet spice shops, though its Hungarian counterpart will do in a pinch (no pun intended).

Chef Pete List (pictured) recommends drizzling the extra vinaigrette—which will keep in the fridge for about two weeks—over Bibb lettuce or brushing it on slices of crusty grilled bread.

(SERVES 4)

For the tartare:

12 ounces fresh Scottish salmon fillet (ask for a center cut), trimmed and skinless
2½ tablespoons finely diced shallots
1½ tablespoons capers
1 teaspoon finely diced sun-dried tomatoes packed in olive oil, plus 1 tablespoon oil from the jar
½ teaspoon minced fresh chives
½ teaspoon minced fresh tarragon
Salt and pepper to taste

For the corn vinaigrette:

2 cups fresh corn kernels
½ small carrot, peeled and sliced
½ leek, thoroughly washed and sliced
¼ fennel bulb, sliced
¼ cup cider vinegar
½ cup water, plus extra as needed
2 cups grapeseed oil
Salt, pepper, and sugar to taste
¼ teaspoon finely chopped fresh thyme

For the haricots verts:

½ pound thin green beans, trimmed
2 tablespoons extra-virgin olive oil
⅛ teaspoon Espelette pepper
¼ teaspoon kosher salt
Juice of ½ lemon

For the herb salad:

Approximately 2 cups baby *mâche* (or other tender lettuce), cleaned and trimmed
4 sprigs fresh dill, trimmed as necessary
Olive oil and Champagne vinegar to taste
4 large, rustic crackers of your choice, or toast points

Special equipment:

3-ounce ring mold

Place a mixing bowl in a larger bowl of ice. With a very sharp knife, slice the salmon into 3 or 4 pieces about ½- to ¼-inch thick and add to the mixing bowl to keep cold. One at a time, dice each piece into tiny cubes, about ⅛-inch square, and place in the bowl; repeat until all the fish is diced. Add the shallots, capers, sun-dried tomatoes and oil, and herbs; check to ensure all the ingredients are fairly uniform in size. Season carefully to taste (very little salt should be required). Keep the mixture cold until ready to plate.

To make the vinaigrette, place all vegetables in a food processor with the vinegar and ½ cup water and blend until smooth. If the mixture is too thick, add more water; it shouldn't quite coat a spoon. With the motor running, slowly add the grapeseed oil to emulsify the dressing; season to taste with salt, pepper, and sugar and add the thyme. Store in the refrigerator until ready to use.

For the *haricots verts*, place a bowl of ice water in the sink. Bring a medium pot of salted water to a roiling boil. Blanch the green beans until bright in color but still al dente (about 1–1½ minutes). Drain the beans from the pot and drop them in the ice water. Once cold, drain the beans again and pat dry with a paper towel. Toss them in a bowl with the olive oil, Espelette pepper, and salt.

Preheat a large cast-iron pan or stovetop griddle over a medium-high burner until it is almost smoking. (Do not add oil.) Add the seasoned beans and char on all sides, then return them to the bowl and add the lemon juice. Keep at room temperature.

Pour vinaigrette carefully onto each of four serving plates to just cover the surface. Place your 3-ounce ring mold in the center of one plate and fill with the salmon *tartare;* gently remove the mold and repeat for the remaining plates. The charred beans can go on top of the salmon in a nice bundle. Finally, arrange about ½ cup *mâche* (or other lettuce) with dill sprigs on each plate, drizzle with oil and vinegar, and serve with crackers or toast points.

LOCAL COOKING BLOGS WE LOVE

Big World | Small Kitchen, bigworldsmallkitchen.com. Keeping one foot in the test kitchen, one in the world of journalism, wunderkind Kazia Jankowski has penned an online recipe collection that's as proficient as it is personable. Look for Peruvian and Polish recipes in particular.

Boulder Locavore, boulderlocavore.com. Lively commentary and lovely photos are Toni Dash's stock in gluten-free trade.

Christopher Cina: A Chef and His Camera, christophercina.com. The pro toque who took the photos for this book maintains his very own gorgeous recipe blog.

Creative Culinary, creative-culinary.com. Barbara Kiebel has garnered a huge following far beyond state lines for her highly polished, constantly updated online cookbook. We're especially fond of her cocktail recipes.

Fork and Pen, forkandpen.com. Also the editor of Eater.com's Denver newsfeed (denver.eater.com), Andra Zeppelin combines refreshingly frank, relatable prose with step-by-step snapshots of her (admittedly infrequent) escapades in the kitchen.

From Argentina with Love, fromargentinawithlove.typepad.com. When Littleton native Rebecca Caro married an Argentine, she married his culture, too. Intimately exploring her adopted homeland's culinary tradition while taking forays into Colorado-Latin fusion (think bison empanadas), Caro's blog also provides information about the cooking classes she leads around town.

Grace(full) Plate, gracefullplate.com. Restaurant news and reviews supplement the recipes on Boulderite Grace Boyle's wide-ranging blog.

Blueberry-and-Lemon Curd Pain Perdu with Buttermilk Ice Cream & Lavender Sugar

Note that this recipe—which List calls "a beautifully simple dessert or a nice brunch item, served with whipped cream instead of ice cream"—requires a day's advance preparation, although he adds that all items will keep for at least a couple of weeks if tightly wrapped or enclosed and stored properly (the lemon curd in the refrigerator, the ice cream in the freezer, the bread in either; there will be leftovers). Lavender is easily available at specialty spice retailers—and if you can find them in season (that is, late summer), huckleberries provide a charming alternative to blueberries.

(SERVES 8)

For the ice cream:

1½ cups heavy cream
1½ tablespoons white peppercorns
6 egg yolks
1 teaspoon salt
½ cup sugar
½ cup buttermilk
½ tablespoon cracked black peppercorns

For the pain perdu:

1 cup whole milk
1 cup goat's milk
½ ounce fresh compressed yeast
¾ cup sugar
1 pound all-purpose flour, divided, plus extra for dusting
6 egg yolks
¼ pound (½ cup) melted butter
1 tablespoon salt
Zest from 1 large lemon
1 cup fresh blueberries
Cooking spray

For the lemon curd:

1 cup lemon juice
¼ cup sugar
½ pound (1 cup) butter
10 egg yolks

For the sugar:

1 tablespoon lavender
Pinch of salt
½ cup granulated sugar

For the batter:

2 cups milk
1 cup flour
¼ cup sugar
4 eggs
1 teaspoon vanilla extract
1 teaspoon salt
1 tablespoon butter

For garnish:

Generous handful of blueberries
8 basil leaves

Special equipment:

ice cream maker
stand mixer (optional)
double boiler (optional)
2 (8 x 4-inch) loaf pans
spice grinder or coffee mill

To make the ice cream: In a pot over medium-high heat, bring the heavy cream and the peppercorns up to a boil, then turn the heat off and steep for 15 minutes. In the meantime, whisk the egg yolks, salt, and sugar gently, so as not to incorporate too much air, in a large bowl until the sugar has dissolved; add the buttermilk. Once the cream has steeped, bring it back to a boil, remove it from the heat, and strain it slowly over the egg mixture, stirring with a wooden spoon so the eggs do not scramble. Stir in the cracked peppercorns and cool. Freeze in ice cream maker according to the manufacturer's instructions.

To make the *pain perdu:* In a pot over low heat, warm the two types of milk together until tepid; turn heat off and let sit for a minute. Add the yeast and sugar to the bowl of your stand mixer if you have one or, if not, to a large mixing bowl and pour the milks over them. Allow the mixture to form a sponge; it should start to foam within 5–10 minutes. At that point, add half the flour, then attach the dough hook to your mixer and mix slowly, or gently mix with a wooden spoon, until you get a loose dough. Add yolks, butter, and salt and continue to mix slowly. When combined, add the remaining flour and lemon zest and combine fully with your dough hook, or knead to incorporate with your hands, then transfer to a clean, flour-dusted surface and continue kneading until smooth. (Be careful not to overwork the dough or it will become tough.) Return the dough to the bowl (if necessary) and gently fold in the berries. Cover the bowl with a damp towel and proof the dough for about an hour, until it has doubled its size. Punch down and let rest 10–15 minutes.

While the dough is proofing, make the lemon curd: Fill a large bowl with ice and set aside. Add water to the bottom of a small double boiler until slightly less than half full and place the boiler on the stove (or use a pot over which a stainless steel or Pyrex mixing bowl will fit). Bring the water to a simmer over medium heat. In the top pot or bowl, add the lemon juice, sugar, and butter, and warm until the sugar is dissolved and the butter is melted; add the yolks and stir constantly with a wooden spoon (do not let the eggs scramble) until the mixture coats the back of spoon, about 15 minutes. Remove from heat and cool over the ice bath.

Preheat the oven to 375°F. Prepare two 8 x 4-inch loaf pans with cooking spray and dust with flour. Fill each halfway with the proofed dough. Make troughs in the top of the dough for the lemon curd and carefully spoon it in, then fold the dough over the curd to cover. Bake for 30 minutes, or until the bread passes the clean toothpick test. Remove from the oven and cool in the pan.

While the bread is baking, make the sugar: Add the lavender and salt to a spice mill or coffee grinder and grind to a coarse powder; add the sugar and grind until uniform.

In a good-size bowl, whisk all the batter ingredients except butter together, making sure there are no lumps. Remove the cooled bread from the loaf pans and slice into about ¾-inch-thick pieces. Soak each in the batter for about a minute. Heat a griddle or large pan to medium-high and add butter to melt (be careful not to burn it). Fry the bread on both sides until the batter is cooked and not squishy, about 2–3 minutes per side. Remove the slices from the pan and slice again on the diagonal. Stack an even number of slices on serving plates, place a scoop of ice cream on top of each stack, dust with the lavender sugar, and garnish with fresh berries and one basil leaf per plate.

BIKER JIM'S GOURMET DOGS

2148 LARIMER STREET
DENVER, CO 80205
(720) 746-9355
BIKERJIMSDOGS.COM
CHEF/OWNER: JIM PITTENGER

What does it say about this city that one of our most famous chefs is a hot dog vendor? Outsiders might infer that we're lacking for culinary diversity or sophistication—but they'd be flat wrong. If anything, it simply says that we here in the erstwhile Wild West cotton to rebels and pioneers—and "Biker Jim" Pittenger fits both bills to a T.

Rolling out his first cart—laden with sausages made of reindeer, rattlesnake, boar, and the like—in 2005, the native Alaskan, former repo man, and longtime motorcycle buff all but single-handedly launched the street-food movement in these parts, well ahead of the national curve. Kudos and numerous TV-camera crews followed—including those of *No Reservations'* Anthony Bourdain—and by early 2011, Pittenger had acquired all the expertise, momentum, and widespread goodwill he needed to open up a brick-and-mortar joint in the Ballpark district. Though he jokes wryly that the neighborhood "is not

completely gentrified—I think it's been six months since there was a murder in the alley," his arrival has clearly accelerated its emergence as a destination.

How a place so bare could have ambience to spare is hard to figure, but it does. Skidmarks darken the concrete floor courtesy of Pittenger's motorcycle buddies. The brick wall's adorned with a mural of his logo: a skull and wieners in lieu of crossbones. Framed photos of tattoos hang beneath a flat-screen TV tuned into the Rockies or Broncos game. Above the glass-paned garage doors that open onto the street, a neon sign flashes YUP or NOPE, rather than OPEN or CLOSED, to indicate business hours, while a blackboard lists the weekly special: Come Thanksgiving, for instance, it might read, "Turducken dog with deconstructed stuffing, turkey gravy, and cranberry chutney." As for the regular menu, game reigns as it always has—there's an elk dog flavored with jalapeño and cheddar, spinach-and-Parmesan-enriched pheasant, cilantro-laced duck. There's a "wiener Wellington" wrapped in puff pastry with mushroom duxelles, Dijon cream, and bordelaise sauce, and a smoked-bacon dog with avocado puree. Toppings range from classic chili to wasabi aioli and caramelized apples; sides include hand-cut chips and deep-fried mac-and-cheese wedges. Naturally the craft brew flows freely (happy hour's "all day, every day"). And there's even dessert—usually ice-cream sandwiches, sometimes cake and pie.

Malaysian Curry Jam

Part of a topping combo that also includes *harissa*-roasted cactus, scallions, and cilantro, this "delicious, slightly spicy, slightly sweet tomato jam is actually suitable for all kinds of meats and grilled veggie dishes," according to Pittenger. It will keep for a couple of weeks under refrigeration.

(MAKES APPROXIMATELY ½ GALLON)

1 tablespoon olive oil

1 medium onion, finely chopped

1½ tablespoons kosher or sea salt, divided

1 cup pineapple chunks (fresh or canned), finely chopped

5 pounds canned crushed tomatoes, preferably organic

½ cup good curry powder, such as Madras

½ cup white wine vinegar

¼ cup brown sugar

Special equipment:

2 or 3 large, wide-mouthed squeeze bottles

Add oil to a large saucepan over medium heat and cook the onion with ½ tablespoon salt until softened; add the pineapple and continue cooking for 1 minute before stirring in the tomatoes. Next, add the curry, vinegar, brown sugar, and remaining tablespoon salt; stir well to combine. Reduce heat to medium-low, partially cover the pan, and simmer for 1 hour.

Let cool and transfer into squeeze bottles; refrigerate until needed.

IRISH CAR BOMB CHEESECAKE

This recipe yields, in Pittenger's words, "one pretty, boozy, and delicious cheesecake to serve 16 people very well—or make 12 people kind of sick." Due to the thickness of the batter, he does not recommend using a hand mixer in lieu of a stand mixer.

(SERVES 12–16)

For the crust:

Shortening for greasing (or use butter)

1¾ cups crushed Oreos or other chocolate sandwich cookie (about 2 packaged sleeves)

⅓–½ cup melted unsalted butter

42 ounces cream cheese, softened to room temperature

1 cup sugar

⅓ cup cornstarch

5 eggs plus 1 egg yolk

½ cup Irish cream liqueur

⅓ cup Irish whiskey

¼ cup Guinness Extra Stout

Special equipment:

9-inch springform pan

kitchen scissors

parchment paper

5-quart stand mixer

Grease a 9-inch springform pan with a small amount of shortening or butter. With your scissors, cut a circle from a piece of parchment paper roughly the size of the bottom of the pan, place it inside, then secure the top of the pan. This should give you a fairly wrinkle-free foundation. Cut a second piece of parchment long enough to encircle the greased inside edge of the pan and trim it so that the paper will stick up from the top by 2–3 inches once affixed.

In a food processor, crush the Oreos to a fine crumb. Transfer to a bowl and stir in ⅓ cup melted butter until well combined; you're looking for a consistency that is not really oily but relatively cohesive (if too dry, add more butter). Press half of the Oreo mixture into the bottom of the pan, the other half along the interior perimeter so it almost reaches the top. Pop into the freezer to chill the crust while you prepare the cake.

Preheat the oven to 350°F. Attach the paddle tool to your stand mixer; add the cream cheese and begin mixing on low speed; add the sugar and mix until well incorporated, a minute or so. Sprinkle in the cornstarch and mix for another minute. Increase the mixing speed and add the eggs (including the yolk), one at a time, making sure each is fully incorporated before adding the next one and scraping the sides of the bowl with a rubber spatula frequently as you go.

Turn the mixer speed to medium and add the cream liqueur and whiskey slowly, so it doesn't splash too much. Transfer ¼ cup cheesecake batter to a small bowl and stir in the Guinness; retrieve your springform pan and pour the remaining batter into the pan. Pour the Guinness mixture over the top in dribs and drabs and, using a knife or spatula, swirl it into a cool design.

Bake for 15 minutes, then reduce the temperature to 200°F and bake for 1 hour and 25 minutes. Turn off the heat and leave the cake in the oven to cool; it should firm up without cracking. At this point, Pittenger likes to freeze his cheesecakes in the pan so they're easy to slice and store; once frozen, they may be dislodged, wrapped tightly in plastic, and returned to the freezer until ready to eat.

Bistro Vendôme

1420 Larimer Street
Denver, CO 80202
(303) 825-3232
BISTROVENDOME.COM
Chef/Co-Owner: Jennifer Jasinski; Co-Owner: Beth Gruitch
Chef de Cuisine: Dana Rodriguez

Sunlight streams through the lace-curtained windows of the yellow-walled dining room and across the mosaic-tiled floor, glinting off a beveled mirror here, silverware on an antique sideboard there. Wood-paddled ceiling fans turn slowly. Around the corner, a snug, zinc-topped bar marks the low-lit entrance; the French doors opposite open onto a flagstone-lined patio bedecked with flower boxes and shaded by a light-strung tree. It's enough to whisk you back to some Parisian cafe circa 1935; you can half see the smoke of Gauloises curling from the ashtrays of gents in fedoras and ladies in flared skirts as they perch with glasses of pastis, waiting for their train to pull into the depot next door.

This is Bistro Vendôme. Tucked into a quiet courtyard off Larimer Square, the flagship of powerhouse partners Jennifer Jasinski and Beth Gruitch remains, after a decade in business, their biggest secret, if only because its siblings across the way, Rioja (page 160) and Euclid Hall (page 61), see more sidewalk traffic. And that's just fine by locals, who take the tagline—"RENDEZVOUS DES AMIS"—to heart.

Here you'll find them lingering over such *plats tres français* as *tartare de boeuf* and *escargots à la moëlle. Blanquette de lapin,* and the occasional special of *canard à l'orange.* Baskets of croissants and smoked-trout omelets come brunch. And, *bien sûr,* bottles of wine from the all-French list—a Bourgogne blanc, perhaps, or Chinon from the Loire Valley, or even a Provençal rosé if they're feeling frisky. Maybe they'll end with a glass of Sauternes or a banana-stuffed crêpe in Cognac sauce. And then they'll just lean back and take it all in, mesmerized by the faraway feeling—*à bout de souffle,* if you will. Do join them.

Roast Chicken with Herbed Jus, Cauliflower Gratin & Mâche Salad in Tarragon Vinaigrette

(SERVES 4)

For the gratin:

1 head cauliflower, cleaned and leaves removed
Salt as directed
2 ounces (4 tablespoons) unsalted butter
¼ cup chopped shallots
1½ cups heavy cream
1 sprig Italian parsley
1 sprig thyme
1 bay leaf
1 teaspoon prepared horseradish
1 teaspoon curry powder
Pinch of freshly grated nutmeg
Pepper to taste
1 cup grated swiss Emmentaler cheese
¼ cup panko bread crumbs

For the chicken:

2 (2–3 pound) chickens or 1 large fatted hen, room temperature
2 ounces (4 tablespoons) olive oil or butter
2 cloves garlic, chopped
1 tablespoon fresh thyme, chopped
2 tablespoons kosher salt
2 teaspoons freshly ground black pepper
Carrot sticks for baking, optional

For the salad:

2 ounces Champagne vinegar
1 tablespoon Dijon mustard
1 tablespoon fresh tarragon, chopped
Pinch of sugar
6 ounces (¾ cup) olive oil
Kosher salt and freshly ground pepper to taste
4 heads *mâche,* cleaned and dried

For the herbed jus:

1 ounce (2 tablespoons) olive oil
1 shallot, sliced
2 cloves garlic, roughly chopped
8 ounces (1 cup) chicken stock
2 ounces (about 4 tablespoons) veal demi-glace (can be substituted with more stock)
1 sprig thyme, chopped
2 fresh Italian parsley sprigs, chopped
2 fresh basil leaves, chopped
2 ounces (4 tablespoons) butter
Salt and pepper to taste

Special equipment:

4 (6-ounce) ramekins

Preheat the oven to 375°F.

Prepare an ice bath in a large bowl. Chop the cauliflower into small florets, reserving the stems. Bring a medium-size pot of salted water to a boil; add the florets and blanch about 3 minutes, then drain and shock them in the ice bath. In a food processor, grind the reserved stems.

Place butter in a large sauté pan over gentle heat, then sweat the shallots until translucent. Add the ground cauliflower stems to the pot and sweat a couple more minutes; add the cream and herbs and cook on low about 10 minutes, until stems are soft. Remove and discard the herbs; blend in the horseradish, curry, and nutmeg and season with salt and pepper to taste. Stir in the blanched cauliflower and adjust the seasonings. Portion into four 6-ounce ramekins and sprinkle with even amounts cheese and bread crumbs. Bake for about 15 minutes or until the tops are browned. (You can make this a day in advance if you prefer, as it reheats well.)

Turn the oven to 325°F. Rub the chicken(s) all over with the oil or butter, garlic, and thyme, then season evenly with salt and pepper. Place in a large baking dish (chef de cuisine Dana Rodriguez, pictured on page 18, recommends setting it atop a few carrot sticks, if desired, so it won't stick to the bottom). Roast for about 30 minutes.

Meanwhile, make the vinaigrette for the salad: In a large bowl, whisk together the vinegar, mustard, tarragon, and sugar. Slowly whisk in the oil, season to taste, and set aside. Trim the *mâche* and store in refrigerator.

Increase the oven temperature to 450°F. (If you have premade the gratin, return the ramekins to the oven at this point to reheat.) Baste the chicken with any drippings and continue roasting another 20 minutes or so—but check it regularly by pricking the thigh with a fork; when the juice runs clear, it's done. (If it's overcooked, the meat will dry out.)

Meanwhile, prepare the herbed jus: Heat the olive oil over medium heat in a medium saucepan and sauté the shallot and garlic a few minutes until light golden. Add the stock and demi-glace, lower heat to a simmer, and reduce by half. Finish with herbs and whisk in the butter to emulsify. Season to taste.

Cut the chicken(s) in half or into pieces as desired and place on a serving platter or divide among four plates. Top with jus and *mâche* tossed in tarragon vinaigrette; serve the ramekins of cauliflower gratin on the side.

THE BITTER BAR

835 WALNUT STREET
BOULDER, CO 80302
(303) 442-3050
THEBITTERBAR.COM
OWNERS: DAVE QUERY AND JAMES LEE

Stopping by this quasi hideaway at the far west end of Walnut Street is like crashing the coolest house party ever (especially if you go the speakeasy route by entering through the unmarked back door). Settees, curtain-lined booths, and a snug bar divide the dimly lit, L-shaped interior into conversation nooks where the young and naturally hip cozy up in twos and threes, surrounded by wink-wink retro knickknacks: an old wooden umbrella

skeleton repurposed as a chandelier and a bank of movie-theater seats here, a vintage typewriter and an antique stove there. In warm weather, the festivities spill out onto the light-strung patio, fueled by the killer libations that are The Bitter Bar's calling card.

As the name suggests, house-made bitters infused with rosemary, grapefruit rind, vanilla bean, and so on are a special point of pride, but co-owner James Lee (himself named one of the nation's top-ten bartenders by *Playboy* in 2009) insists that everything his crew serves, potable or edible, is crafted "with particular attention to quality and integrity. No detail is overlooked," from flavored syrups and ice cubes to charcuterie cured on-site and fresh-baked bread. The concise, gastropubby menu bears out his claim. Crunchy, greaseless jalapeño poppers are hot, hot, haute stuffed with duck confit and smoked Gouda alongside onion-smacked ranch dressing; mussels come steamed with sausage and fennel in no mere broth but rather rich lobster bisque; the scent of cinnamon and vanilla bean wafts from warm, gooey s'mores. Of course, the cocktails lead the charge, featuring small-batch, often locally distilled spirits and all manner of inventive twists, be it a splash of cayenne maple syrup or *kombucha* (fermented tea) or a hint of lavender or thyme; take the award-winning Amber Wave, blending mezcal, *amaro,* ginger liqueur, and *verjus* (unripe grape juice), plus those house bitters, to startling effect. "The staff is made up of some of the most passionate and creative bartenders I've had the privilege of working with," says Lee (pictured), and the proof is in the pudding—or the proper glassware, as the case may be.

DEATH ON THE BEARSKIN RUG

Fairly new on the market, bright-red Hum is a strong liqueur flavored with hibiscus, ginger, cardamom, and Kaffir lime.

(SERVES 1)

1 ounce Hum Botanical Spirit
¼ ounce absinthe (Lee recommends
    Denver's own Leopold Bros.)
½ ounce agave nectar
½ ounce fresh lemon juice
3–4 ounces hot water
Orange twist for garnish

Add all liquids to a 12- to 14-ounce mug and stir to mix. Garnish with an orange twist.

Bittersweet

500 East Alameda Avenue
Denver, CO 80209
(303) 942-0320
bittersweetdenver.com
Chef/Co-Owner: Olav Peterson; Co-Owner: Melissa Severson

This heavily trafficked, low-rent stretch of Alameda Boulevard is one of the last places you'd expect to find a dining destination as tranquil and suave as Bittersweet. But here it is: Olav Peterson's vision of a twinkling farmhouse impeccably realized against a backdrop of neon commotion. Flanked by kitchen gardens and a sumac-shaded patio, the two-room venue juxtaposes salvaged wood and marble elements, antique cabinets and cowhide-covered chairs, glass pendant lamps, and shades of gray that, says Peterson, "look so different as the light changes" to set a supremely inviting mood, proportionately rustic and urbane.

By the same token, Peterson's twofold commitment to raw material and highly polished product reveals itself dish by dish. In autumn, he might be seeding his front-

yard plots with kale and chard to "clip right away and use as microgreens, or nurture to maturity" for the winter menu; come April, "we'll start planting beans, peas, tomatoes, squashes, and lettuces." But whatever the season, those humble pickings undergo a remarkable transformation in the kitchen to yield such refinements as fried-oyster po' boys atop puff pastry with remoulade foam, pickled cucumbers, and bacon cracklings; chicken-noodle soup turned graceful duo of *poussin* and celery-root *agnolotti* in thyme broth; or lavender-scented ricotta cheesecake garnished with lemon curd, honeyed figs, and almond lace. The wine list is likewise clever yet sincere in its emphasis on such lesser-known regions as the Savoie and the Mosel in France and Germany, respectively; Washington's Yakima Valley; and Tokaji, Hungary. In effect, a visit to Bittersweet renders you a happy armchair agrotourist.

Seared Rockfish with Warm Crab-Kale Salad & Vanilla Consommé

Though he favors rockfish (better known as striped bass) for the sweetness its flesh derives from its diet of crustaceans, Peterson suggests tilapia as a substitute. He also notes that while clarifying consommé with gelatin takes longer than the raft method—you will need about two days to do it—"it's more foolproof" (especially if you use a digital scale, as is highly recommended). There may be some left over; if so, it will keep about five days. Since it "isn't unlike the broth in a Thai hot pot," you could heat up the remainder with noodles and Asian vegetables.

(SERVES 4)

For the vanilla consommé:

1–2 teaspoons cooking oil (Peterson likes rice-bran oil)
Seeds of 4 vanilla beans
2 shallots, finely chopped
1 clove garlic, chopped
1 tablespoon crushed red pepper
2 quarts chicken stock
Sheet gelatin (amount determined as directed)

Approximately 2 tablespoons rice-bran or other cooking oil
4 large king crab legs, split and shelled, meat cut into 3-inch pieces
1 bunch Tuscan kale, cleaned and chopped
4 cloves garlic, sliced paper thin with sharp knife
4 (4–5 ounce) rockfish fillets

Special equipment:
two large, heat-safe plastic containers
digital scale
coffee filter

To make the consommé, heat oil (as little as possible) in a good-size saucepan over a medium-high burner and sauté the vanilla, shallots, garlic, and crushed red pepper. Add stock and bring to a boil.

Place a plastic container large enough to contain the infused stock on your digital scale and set it to zero, then pour the stock into the container to determine its weight in grams. Multiply the number by 0.05; the sum will equal the amount of gelatin you need in grams. Measure the gelatin accordingly, then bloom it by soaking it in a bowl filled with ice-cold water for 3–5 minutes. Add the bloomed gelatin to the stock, place the mixture back into the pot, and return to a boil; transfer it to the container and freeze overnight.

Place a sieve lined with a coffee filter over another, larger plastic container; uncover the container of frozen stock and place it upside down atop the filter so that, as it melts, it drips through. This process will take about 24 hours in the refrigerator.

To complete the recipe, place about 8 ounces consommé in a small pot and warm through over gentle heat. Meanwhile, divide the 2 tablespoons oil between two saucepans over medium-high heat. In one, sauté the crab, kale, and garlic until warm; in the other, sear the rockfish fillets until cooked through, about 5 minutes on one side and 3 on the other.

Distribute even amounts of the crab-kale mixture in a mound at the center of each of four large, shallow serving bowls; top with fish. Ladle a small amount of consommé around the warm salad and serve immediately.

Maple-Cured Duck Ham with Fall Fruit Salad & Smoked Raisin Vinaigrette

Begin the curing process at least a day in advance. Good spice retailers should carry pink sea salt and maple sugar. There will be extra vinaigrette, but it should keep for some time under refrigeration.

(SERVES 6)

For the duck ham:

450 grams (about 1½ cups) kosher salt
50 grams (about 2¾–3 tablespoons) pink sea salt
225 grams (about 1⅛ cups) granulated sugar
6 duck breasts, skin on
100 grams (about ½ cup) maple sugar

For the vinaigrette:

2-pound block of ice (freezing water in a plastic
   container works nicely)
1 cup golden raisins
1 shallot, peeled
3 cloves garlic, peeled
3 tablespoons Champagne vinegar
2½ cups olive oil

For the fruit salad:

Granulated sugar and water as directed
2 small, firm-fleshed apples, scooped with a small baller
2 small, firm-fleshed pears, scooped with a small baller
1 large cucumber, peeled, seeded, quartered, and thinly
   sliced lengthwise into ribbons

Special equipment:

digital scale
wood chips, preferably hickory
outdoor smoker
two-piece pan (perforated and base) for smoker
meat thermometer

First, cure the duck. Mix salts and sugar in a large bowl. (Though we have provided volume equivalents for the cure ingredients, Peterson advises the use of a digital scale to measure them in grams.) Generously coat duck breasts on all sides in the mixture, place in a large, nonreactive (plastic or glass) container, and refrigerate, covered, for 24 hours.

While the duck is curing, begin the vinaigrette by preparing your smoker (Peterson uses hickory chips, though any kind will do). Place ice block in a perforated pan and set it over a base pan; when the smoker is emitting low heat, add the double pan and smoke the ice for about 30 minutes. Remove and allow any remaining ice to melt. ("All we're making is liquid smoke," explains Peterson.) Place ¾ cup of the resulting smoked water in a blender with the raisins, shallot, garlic, and vinegar and blend on high speed until smooth; add oil slowly to emulsify. Reserve.

Next, prepare a simple syrup for the fruit salad. In a medium-size pot, bring to a boil an equal amount of sugar and water sufficient to cover the apples and pears; add the fruit and poach until just tender, about 7 minutes. Remove from syrup and store in refrigerator until needed, along with the cucumber.

To smoke the duck, rinse breasts well and sprinkle maple sugar evenly on the fatty sides. Add wood chips to your smoker along with the breasts and smoke to an internal temperature of 155°F (check with a thermometer; starting cold, this should take a couple of hours).

Cool the meat in the refrigerator, then slice very thin. Dot the surface of a (preferably rectangular) serving platter with slices of duck, fruit balls, cucumber ribbons, and dollops of vinaigrette to create an artistic pattern.

Blackbelly Catering

BLACKBELLYCATERING.COM
CHEFHOSEA.COM
CHEF/OWNER: HOSEA ROSENBERG

Ask New Mexico transplant Hosea Rosenberg what sets his catering company apart, and he'll tell you about his five-acre farm just south of Longmont: "We raise our own heritage-breed pigs and lamb; we have a chicken coop and a greenhouse. We're trying very hard to run a self-sustaining, organic operation." He'll also allude to an air of exclusivity:

"We position ourselves as a high-end, boutique catering company. I retain mixologists and sommeliers on staff and aim for five-star cuisine."

Although such conscientious branding may well contribute to his success, let's face it—more than a few clients are undoubtedly swayed by his celebrity. While serving as executive chef of Jax Fish House & Oyster Bar (page 83)—a job he held from 2004 to 2010—Rosenberg not only competed on Season 5 of Bravo's popular *Top Chef* series but emerged as the winner.

Loads of charisma are a must for any TV personality, of course, and Rosenberg shines when he appears at area pop-up dinners and food festivals. But fans are still waiting for him to parlay all that name recognition into square footage and open an actual restaurant. "For the past two years I've been hunting for a spot," he says, "but I'm really busy—and really picky about finding the right location." Well, until that day comes, the following recipe should tide them over.

SMOKED RAINBOW TROUT SALAD WITH GREEN CHILE–CORNBREAD PUDDING

For convenience, roast the chiles in advance by placing them directly over the flame of a gas burner or under a hot broiler and rotating them until completely blackened. Place in a bowl and cover with plastic wrap until cool; the charred skins should peel or crumble away easily.

(SERVES 4)

For the cornbread pudding:

4 whole eggs plus 2 yolks
1 cup buttermilk
1 cup flour
1 cup cornmeal
¾ cup sugar
¾ teaspoon baking soda
¾ teaspoon salt, plus extra to taste
½ pound (1 cup) butter, melted, plus extra
    butter for greasing the pan
1 cup cream
1 cup milk
2 roasted, peeled, destemmed, deseeded,
    and chopped Hatch green chiles
1 roasted, peeled, destemmed, deseeded,
    and chopped poblano chile
1 tablespoon chopped cilantro
Black pepper, cayenne pepper, and cumin to taste

For the salad:

1 pound fresh boneless rainbow trout fillets, skin on
Salt and black pepper to taste
½ green apple, peeled and diced very small
½ fennel bulb, diced very small
¼ red onion, diced very small
2 tablespoons mayonnaise
1 tablespoons sour cream
Zest and juice of 2 lemons
1 teaspoon whole-grain mustard
1 teaspoon minced fresh chives
1 teaspoon minced fresh parsley
Cayenne pepper to taste

For garnish:

1 head frisée, trimmed and tossed in a little
    olive oil and salt
12 sprigs fresh cilantro
1 lime, cut into quarters
½ cup pine nuts, toasted quickly in a small,
    dry pan or in a 350° F oven for about 10 minutes

Special equipment:

outdoor smoker
1 (6 x 6-inch) baking pan
4 jumbo muffin cups or 8-ounce ceramic ramekins

Preheat the oven to 350°F. To make the pudding, break 2 eggs into a small mixing bowl, add buttermilk, and whisk until well mixed. In another, larger bowl, combine the flour, cornmeal, sugar, baking soda, and ¾ teaspoon salt. Slowly whisk in the egg mixture until just combined; stir in melted butter. Grease a 6 x 6-inch baking pan, pour in the batter, and bake about 45 minutes, or until the cornbread is firm and an inserted toothpick comes out clean. Cool completely, then dice the bread into small cubes.

While the pudding is cooling, make the salad. First, prepare your smoker. Once hot, season trout on both sides with salt and black pepper and smoke until the fish is just cooked through— about 5–10 minutes. Remove skin and let cool. When ready to handle, flake trout into a bowl with fingers and set aside.

In another, large bowl, place all remaining salad ingredients except cayenne pepper and mix well to integrate. Add the trout and mix carefully, trying not to break up the trout too much. Season to taste with cayenne as well as salt and black pepper; then chill for at least 1 hour.

Meanwhile, finish the pudding. Turn the oven down to 325°F and fill jumbo muffin molds or ramekins with cornbread cubes. In a large bowl, combine well remaining 2 whole eggs, yolks, cream, milk, chiles, and cilantro, along with black and cayenne peppers and cumin to taste. Pour the mixture over the cubes until containers are completely filled and the cornbread has soaked up the liquid. (If there is enough cornbread and egg mixture left over, by all means make more puddings; they freeze well after baking.)

Fill a large, shallow glass baking dish with warm water, gently set the molds in it, and place it on the oven's center rack. Cook, uncovered, for 35–40 minutes or until puddings are set but jiggly to the touch (there should be no runny liquid in the centers). Allow to cool at room temperature; then run a small knife around the sides of the molds or ramekins and gently pop out the puddings.

To serve, place one pudding off the center of each of four plates, then lay a generous ½ cup of trout salad in a line alongside it. Divide garnish evenly among plates, sprinkling the pine nuts atop the fish.

Black Cat Farm~Table~Bistro

1964 13th Street
Boulder, CO 80302
(303) 444-5500
blackcatboulder.com
Chef/Co-Owner: Eric Skokan
Co-Owner: Jill Skokan

In an era when the provenance of every last lentil and parsley leaf is earnestly documented on every last menu, it's easy to grow jaded about all the locavore movement hath wrought—until you come to a place like Black Cat Bistro in downtown Boulder. Eric Skokan doesn't just talk the talk and walk the walk between pasture and plate; he plants the plants and herds the herds himself on a sprawling nearby farm—many of them heirloom crops and heritage breeds that he not only features prominently on the menu of his swank flagship and that of adjacent gastropub Bramble & Hare (1970 13th Street; 303-444-9110; brambleandhare.com) but also sells through CSAs and the local farmers' market.

What Skokan doesn't do is hew to the popular but somewhat disingenuous philosophy that quality ingredients should speak for themselves. Absent the fetish for homestyle simplicity, this is epicurean fare: chefly in conception, painterly in presentation, ever-changing. On one visit, you may find lamb tartare garnished with candied currant tomatoes, sunchoke chips, and a swirl of rose yogurt; on the next, cabbage stuffed with wild rice and bathed in foraged mushroom–apple broth, followed by chocolate beignets with tomato-basil jam. Next door, there might be chickpea fritters in lime vinaigrette or, if you're lucky, the unforgettable smoked Mulefoot rib over pork-skin noodles in Sichuan-spiced jus.

The young crew behind both bars is no less ambitious. Black Cat's wine program, heavy on boutique and biodynamic producers, is among our favorites on the entire Front Range; we can always count on falling in love with a discovery from Alto Adige or the Wachau. Bramble & Hare focuses, as you might expect, on saisons, fruit ales, and other craft brews both local and imported. And seasonal cocktails like the following are *au courant*—not to mention much easier to prepare at home than might be, say, strudel made from the leg of a duck you raised yourself.

THE FALL ALSO RISES

Cynar is an Italian *amaro*, or bittersweet herbal liqueur. Don't let its defining ingredient, artichoke, deter you—the flavor is surprisingly smooth and rich. Credit for this recipe goes to bartender Jennifer O'Brien.

Angostura bitters can be used in lieu of The Bitter Truth brand (which is available online at the-bitter-truth.com).

(SERVES 1)

1½ ounces Cynar
½ ounce Bénédictine
½ ounce dry vermouth, such as Dolin
Juice of ½ red grapefruit, plus twist cut from
    peel for garnish
Dash of The Bitter Truth Old-Time Aromatic Bitters

Special equipment:
cocktail shaker

Pre-chill a rocks glass.

Place all ingredients (except the twist) in a shaker with ice, shake lightly, and double strain through a fine-mesh sieve over a large ice cube into your glass. Garnish with the grapefruit twist.

BONES

701 GRANT STREET
DENVER, CO 80203
(303) 860-2929
BONESDENVER.COM
CHEF/OWNER: FRANK BONANNO; CHEF: MATTHEW LEWIS

Though it's tucked smack between his flagship destinations at the edge of Capitol Hill—
Mizuna (225 East 7th Avenue; 303-832-4778; mizunadenver.com) and Luca d'Italia (711
Grant Street; 303-832-6600; lucadenver.com)—the space that now contains this most
idiosyncratic of noodle bars was long easy for chef-owner Frank Bonanno to overlook.
"It was a sad, rundown slice of sandwich shop," he recalls, "but the realtor asked that I
ignore its grime and ugliness because it had 'such lovely bones.' From those words on,
everything clicked. Bones are lovely, you know; they're so . . . promising. I saw a menu
full of deceptively simple broths made the old-fashioned way—for hours and hours,
beginning with the roasting of bones. Opulent ingredients—escargot, lobster, suckling
pig—rendered familiar by virtue of a humble soup bowl and a fat bunch of noodles. In that
tight little room," he adds, "there's something exotic in the everyday, something luxurious
in the economy of a daily-changing menu that's offered up on a single sheet of paper."

   Not to mention something festive in the crush and clamor of patrons knocking back
sake cocktails over shared plates of duck-sausage egg rolls and exquisite roasted bone
marrow. Not to mention something decidedly global sprouting from the signature soups'

Asian roots, as fennel and macadamia nuts, brussels sprouts and red *kuri* squash bob in coconut, plum-soy, or miso broth brimming with rice, egg, or buckwheat noodles and topped with lump crab or shredded pork shoulder. Nor to mention something new wave in the very nostalgia of house-made soft-serve ice cream, whose ever-changing flavors range from *horchata* to vanilla-bacon to chocolate-cherry cola.

No bones about it—this joint's got guts.

Escargot Potstickers

(MAKES 35-40)

For the filling:

1 stick unsalted butter at room temperature

3 cloves garlic, finely minced

4 tablespoons lemon juice

1 bunch Italian parsley, chopped

1 tablespoon salt

1 teaspoon pepper

28 ounces canned escargot

2 eggs

1 (16-ounce) package round *gyoza* wrappers

Vegetable oil as directed

2 tablespoons chopped garlic

1 tablespoon chopped ginger

¼–½ cup water

1 tablespoon butter

1 teaspoon salt

1 teaspoon Korean red pepper

3 tablespoons lemon juice

To make the filling, place the butter, garlic, lemon juice, parsley, salt, and pepper in a food processor and puree until smooth, about 3 minutes. Drain and rinse escargot; pat dry with paper towel. Add escargot to the processor bowl and pulse several times to incorporate, ensuring that the snails aren't chopped too fine.

Crack the eggs into a bowl and whisk. Lay the wrappers out on a clean cutting board (8–10 at a time). Brush the tops with the egg wash and place a small spoonful of filling in the centers. Fold the wrappers in half to create a half-moon shape and press to seal the edges. Repeat until all the wrappers are used.

Place a 10-inch sauté pan over medium-high heat. Add just enough vegetable oil to coat the bottom (about ¼ cup, though chef Matthew Lewis, pictured, emphasizes that you may need less); when it's very hot, add the first batch of potstickers (about a dozen at a time to avoid overcrowding). Crisp on one side until golden brown, then flip over and crisp the other side. Remove to drain on paper towels. Discard the oil, clean out the pan, add the minimum amount of oil required to coat, and repeat the process with the remaining potstickers. Once the last batch is finished, reduce heat to medium and add to the clean pan a tiny bit of oil, then the garlic and ginger. Cook for roughly 2 minutes (do not brown); deglaze with water. Finally, mount in the butter, stirring constantly to form a sauce.

Remove the potstickers to a serving platter. Whisk salt, red pepper, and lemon juice into the sauce and pour over the potstickers. Serve immediately.

Cafe Aion

1235 Pennsylvania Avenue
Boulder, CO 80302
(303) 993-8131
cafeaion.com
Chef/Owner: Dakota Soifer

Cafe Aion has the restaurant's equivalent of an old soul, exuding thoughtfulness and poise against all expectation after only a few years in business—not least given its location on Boulder's rowdy college corner, The Hill. In part, of course, it's inherited—the patina of age on brick walls and wood floors mellowed by the sunlight that streams through the bay windows of this long-standing boardinghouse turned bookstore, whose name (and painted logo) the young owners naturally adopted: "Honestly," says chef Dakota Soifer, "it was, 'What are going to call this place?—Oh, look there's a big sign on the wall!' How better to tie it into a neighborhood where long-timers would have that recognition and nostalgia?" But the sense of place that fills the tiny dining room is enhanced by design, he adds: "My original partners and I built everything—the tabletops, this bar. We spent days figuring out how to get corrugated steel to rust. And we all felt good about putting the sweat in ourselves."

Meanwhile, almost by accident, they took a similarly Old World approach to the food and drink. "We thought we'd be this bar with good snacks," explains Soifer, but "suddenly

we're taking reservations, and we're like, 'We've just got this scrap of paper for a menu, and people think we're a restaurant!'" So they expanded the selection of small plates to include charcuterie boards and larger platters for sharing, and added daytime hours to serve pastries and other brunch items. "We're a small operation," he says, "but if we're going to do something, we want to do it ourselves. At Zuni Café [the San Francisco institution where he got his start], Judy Rodgers's thing was, 'Stop, wait, let's make this *more* difficult. What will add more interest and depth of flavor?' We bake our own baguettes, hand-roll croissants, cure our own meats."

Infusing such house-made and locally sourced ingredients with the flavors of Spain and North Africa—"I love the exotic quality of olives and wild seeds, coriander and cinnamon"—the former student of architecture has built a repertoire that's intensely redolent of the Moorish Mediterranean. Sausages and salted fish, dried fruits and nuts, ancient grains and spice mixtures abound among the tapas and *mezze,* in *tagines* and paellas; though small and not strictly Spanish, the wine list also captures the Iberian spirit in the form of native varietals like Godello, Macabeo, and Tinta de Toro. And while it may all be a shade too mature for pizza-pounding CU freshmen, that's just as well for their professors. Take this as high praise: Aion's for the quiet, the cultured—even, yes, the bookish.

Braised Oxtail with Figs & Chickpeas

Says Soifer, "This recipe is labor intensive, requiring three days of preparation. But the results are totally worth the effort. It's a really fun dish to take the weekend to cook and enjoy with friends on a cozy Sunday evening. We like to serve it over steaming couscous or with grilled pita (or even grilled pizza dough) for scooping. Once you feel comfortable with the techniques involved, you can use this recipe as a template for cooking lamb shanks or duck legs as well."

Preserved lemons can be found at specialty gourmet shops and through online retailers.

(SERVES 6)

2 pounds oxtails

½ teaspoon ground coriander

Salt and pepper to taste

2 tablespoons olive oil

6 whole shallots, peeled

3 carrots, roll cut

8 cloves garlic, roughly chopped

12 cardamom pods

2 *chiles de arbol* or similar dried pepper

1 sprig rosemary

1 cinnamon stick

1 teaspoon tomato paste

½ cup red wine

1 quart beef stock

2 cups cooked, drained chickpeas

1 cup dried, halved figs

¼ cup fresh cilantro leaves, chopped

1 tablespoon preserved lemon, chopped

On day one, cut the oxtails into pieces that will fit easily into a large dish and season with coriander, salt, and pepper. Cover with plastic and refrigerate.

On day two, preheat the oven to 325°F. Select a lidded braising pot that is just big enough to hold the oxtails in a single layer. Add olive oil and bring almost to the smoking point over medium-high heat; then add meat and sear to a dark golden, about 4–5 minutes per side. Remove the meat from the pot and stir in the shallots and carrots. After 2 minutes, toss in the garlic, cardamom, chiles, rosemary, and cinnamon, allowing them to toast and become aromatic. After an additional 5 minutes, stir in the tomato paste to coat and allow it to lightly caramelize. Add the wine, stir vigorously, and then add the stock. Return the oxtails to the pot and bring the whole mixture to a simmer. Put the lid on the pot and place it in the oven.

After 2 hours, check the meat; it should be quite tender, almost falling off the bone. Let the pot cool to room temperature and then refrigerate overnight. (As the meat rests in the braising liquid, it will absorb more flavor.)

On day three, let the pot sit out to bring it to room temperature, or warm slightly over low heat. Remove the oxtails and pick the meat off the bone, discarding tough and fatty bits. Strain the braising liquid into a smaller pot; add the picked meat, chickpeas, and figs to the liquid. Taste mixture for salt, add more if needed, and heat through over a low burner. Serve topped with cilantro and preserved lemon.

Braised Octopus with Olives & Cilantro

"This is one of my favorite winter tapas," says Soifer. "The flavors are so bold and warming. We serve it with a nice grilled flatbread—pita is perfect for mopping up the juices—but you could also spoon it over saffron rice for a great entree. I love pairing it with a shot of *ouzo* [Greek anisette] or a glass of Fino Sherry."

(SERVES 6)

4 tablespoons olive oil, divided

2 pounds whole baby octopus

6 cloves garlic, sliced thinly

3 *chiles de arbol* or similar dried pepper

½ preserved lemon, julienned (see preceding headnote)

1 large sprig rosemary

5 cups canned tomatoes, crushed

¼ cup kalamata olives, pitted

1 cup cooked chickpeas

2 teaspoons salt

2 tablespoons chopped fresh cilantro leaves

Preheat the oven to 375°F.

Heat 1 tablespoon olive oil in a large, heavy-bottomed (preferably cast-iron) frying pan over high heat until almost smoking and add half the octopus. (It is very important not to overcrowd the pan, as you are trying to get a good sear and release as much moisture as possible.) After a minute, give the octopus a good stir, let it sear for another minute or so, and place it in a colander in the sink to drain. Wipe the pan clean and repeat with another tablespoon olive oil and the rest of the octopus.

In a 4-quart, lidded casserole dish, heat the remaining 2 tablespoons olive oil over medium heat. Add the garlic, chiles, preserved lemon, and rosemary and stir until the garlic is golden and the mixture is fragrant. Add the tomatoes, olives, chickpeas, salt, and octopus; mix well, cover tightly, and bake for 2 hours.

Scoop into a serving dish, top with freshly chopped cilantro, and enjoy!

Central Bistro & Bar

1691 Central Street
Denver, CO 80211
(303) 477-4582
centralbistrobar.com
Owner: Isiah Salazar; Chef: Gerard Strong

One might have opined, prior to the opening of Central Bistro & Bar in the summer of 2012, that Denver had quite enough contemporary American neighborhood eateries with generic-sounding names to warrant yet another one—especially in LoHi, so close to the saturated downtown market. But one—including myself—would have been wrong. There's always room for a joint with pizzazz.

Gleaming amid creamy-white and bright-orange hues, the dining room also glows in the light of a gigantic neon sign over the open kitchen, reading HOT—the letters salvaged from the former Regency Hotel, now student housing owned by the family of proprietor Isiah Salazar. Message received: Hearty warmth suffuses every inch of the seasonal menu, as the chef pays ample homage to regional comfort foods by sourcing pork from Iowa and cheese from Wisconsin, whipping up New England–style johnnycakes here and Southern-fried pickles there. Yet the effect is hardly down-home: Sophisticated presentation distinguishes everything from a painterly raw-vegetable salad to almond gazpacho poured

tableside over green grapes and basil sorbet. Craft cocktails from the cozy bar are likewise smartly conceived, be it an intriguing blend of blonde ale and Calvados with green apples or a brunch-time pour of gin-spiked, tarragon-scented beet juice.

Here's to a newcomer with a rosy—make that electric-orange—future.

Pork Chops with Peach Barbecue Sauce, White Cheddar Grits & Peach Salad

The following recipes were provided by original chef Lance Barto (pictured). Requiring access to both a grill and a smoker, this one's for the outdoor-cooking enthusiast. Start the pork chops a day in advance, and give yourself a few hours to complete the rest.

You can store the extra barbecue sauce in a plastic container in the refrigerator for up to a week, or in the freezer indefinitely.

(SERVES 4)

For the pork chops:

2 medium shallots, peeled
5 cloves garlic, peeled
½ cup kosher salt
½ cup sugar
12 black peppercorns
4 bay leaves
2 tablespoons mustard seed
2 tablespoons juniper berries
1 teaspoon nutmeg
8 cups warm water
4 (8–10 ounce) bone-in pork rib chops

For the pickled shallots:

6 shallots, peeled
¼ teaspoon salt
1 fluid ounce (2 tablespoons) dry red wine
2 fluid ounces (4 tablespoons) red wine vinegar
2 fluid ounces (4 tablespoons) water
1 tablespoon sugar

For the pickled mustard seeds:

2 tablespoons mustard seeds
¼ cup cider vinegar
1 teaspoon kosher salt
1 teaspoon sugar

For the caramelized onions:

1 tablespoon canola oil
3 white onions, julienned
2 fluid ounces (4 tablespoons) white wine
2 tablespoons kosher salt

For the barbecue sauce:

3 white onions, peeled and halved
3 peaches, peeled and pitted
1 tablespoon canola oil
1 tablespoon wildflower honey, plus extra as necessary
1 tablespoon sherry vinegar, plus extra as necessary
Salt to taste

For the grits:

1 teaspoon canola oil

1 tablespoon minced garlic

1 tablespoon minced shallot

2 cups vegetable or chicken broth

1 cup whipping cream

1 cup milled grits (preferably Anson Mills or Logan Turnpike Mill)

Water as necessary

4 ounces (1 stick) unsalted butter, cut into pieces

¾ cup grated white cheddar cheese

Salt to taste

3 ounces arugula, cleaned and trimmed

1 ripe peach, sliced

1 fluid ounce (2 tablespoons) extra-virgin olive oil

Pinch of kosher salt

Special equipment:

mandoline (optional)

outdoor wood smoker, preferably using applewood chips

outdoor grill

meat thermometer

First, begin the pork chops: In a large mixing bowl, combine all ingredients but pork chops to make a brine (the warm water will help dissolve the salt and sugar). Place in the refrigerator to chill a couple of hours; then immerse chops and refrigerate overnight.

To pickle the shallots: Slice them very thin on a mandoline (or carefully with a sharp knife) and season with salt. Place in a medium-size, nonreactive mixing bowl and allow to soften for 15 minutes. In another bowl, combine the remaining ingredients well to make a brine. Drain any excess moisture from the shallots and pour the brine on top. Cover and store bowl in refrigerator.

Next, prepare the mustard seeds: Bring a small pot of water to a boil over high heat, add the seeds, and boil for 30 seconds. Drain through a fine-meshed strainer, rinse under cold water, and transfer the seeds to a small, nonreactive bowl. Add the vinegar, salt, and sugar to a small pot and bring to a boil over high heat, then pour just enough of the mixture over the seeds to cover. Let cool at room temperature.

To caramelize the onions: Heat oil in a large pan and sauté the onions over low heat. (This can take upward of 30–45 minutes, but it is important to bring out their sweetness rather than their bitterness, so do not increase the heat.). Once they have begun to acquire a deep-brown color, deglaze the pan with white wine; add salt and reserve.

To make the sauce: Prepare your smoker and smoke the onions and peaches for 15 minutes; remove and let cool. Slice the onions thin. Add oil to a large pan and sauté the sliced onion over low heat until it begins to color, about 30 minutes. Add in the peaches, honey, vinegar, and salt and simmer 10–15 minutes. Place in a food processor and blend until smooth. Taste to ensure the flavor is balanced—it should be smoky, sweet, and sour; if need be, adjust with more honey, vinegar, and/or salt.

To prepare the grits: In a large pan with oil over medium-low heat, sauté the garlic and shallot until softened and translucent but not brown, about 2–3 minutes. Add the broth and cream and bring to a simmer; whisk in the grits and cook for 45 minutes at a simmer, whisking constantly to prevent scorching. (If the grits begin to look dry, add water.) Gradually whisk in the butter and the white cheddar and season to taste; then turn heat off, cover, and reserve.

Preheat your grill. Remove the pork chops from the brine and pat dry, then grill to medium (about 142°F internal temperature; if thicker chops begin to darken before centers are fully cooked, finish in a 350°F oven). Transfer to a plate and rest for 4–5 minutes.

To serve: Toss arugula in a bowl with ripe peach slices, olive oil, salt, and the reserved pickled shallots. Spoon warm grits onto the center of each of four serving plates and lay pork chops on top, then drizzle the barbecue sauce in a ring around the grits. Garnish as desired with equal amounts of pickled mustard seeds and caramelized onions; divide the arugula mixture evenly among the plates, setting a handful on top of each pork chop; and serve immediately.

CORN-AND-BACON RISOTTO WITH WISCONSIN CHEESE CURDS & PAPRIKA OIL

The extra garlic and corn purees will keep in the refrigerator for up to a week; the former can be added to salad dressings, pasta sauces, and soups, or used as a bread spread, and the latter make a nice accompaniment to pan-seared scallops.

(SERVES 4)

For the paprika oil:

2 fluid ounces canola oil
1 teaspoon smoked paprika

For the roasted corn:

2 ears sweet corn, shucked
1 tablespoon canola oil
Salt and pepper to taste

For the roasted garlic puree:

2 heads garlic
½ cup canola oil

For the corn puree:

3 ears sweet corn, shucked
1 quart milk
1 bay leaf
1 sprig thyme

For the risotto:

1 quart chicken stock
1 tablespoon canola oil
¼ cup finely diced yellow onion
1 teaspoon minced garlic
1 cup Arborio rice
½ cup white wine
Salt to taste

1 medium red bell pepper, deveined and diced small
¾ cup Wisconsin cheddar curds (available at Whole Foods or specialty markets)
6 strips bacon, cooked until crispy, divided
2 tablespoons chopped chives, divided
Salt and pepper to taste

To make the paprika oil: Pulse the ingredients to combine in a blender, pour into a small container or squeeze bottle, and let sit until the paprika settles. Strain and reserve.

To prepare the roasted corn: Slice the kernels carefully off the cobs with a knife. In a pan with canola oil over medium heat, lightly sauté them until tender, about 3 minutes. Season with salt and pepper.

Next, roast the garlic: Preheat the oven to 300°F. Slice off the tops of the bulbs so the tips of the cloves are showing. Place top-down in a shallow baking pan and pour oil over the top. Cover the pan with aluminum foil and place in oven until tender and golden, about 1 hour. Remove and let cool, reserving the oil in the refrigerator for future use (it's great on bread or in pasta sauce). When ready to handle, press the roasted cloves out of the bulbs and mash them with a fork or use a food processor to grind them into a paste. Set aside.

To make the corn puree: Slice the kernels carefully off the cobs. Add them along with the milk and herbs to a small saucepan and, over medium heat, bring to a simmer. Cook until tender, about 10 minutes. Strain the kernels, reserving the milk (but discarding the herbs); place in a blender and puree, adding the milk as necessary (use as little as possible) until the consistency is smooth. Cover with waxed paper or plastic wrap to prevent the formation of surface skin and set aside.

Begin the risotto: In a medium pot, bring stock to a simmer. Add canola oil to another good-size pot and sweat onion and garlic over medium-low heat. Add rice and toast until translucent; deglaze with white wine. Add ¾ cup stock to the risotto, stirring continuously; when the liquid is almost gone, add another ¾ cup and keep stirring. Repeat until the rice is tender yet still has tooth, about 20–25 minutes. (You will likely use all the stock, though a little less or more may be needed to ensure the proper al dente texture.) Salt to taste.

When the risotto is finished, fold in the roasted corn kernels, 2 tablespoons roasted garlic puree, 4 tablespoons corn puree, diced red pepper, cheddar curds, 4 pieces bacon crumbled into small pieces, and 1 tablespoon chives. Heat a few minutes until the cheese begins to melt. Season to taste. Ladle into four bowls and garnish each with a half piece of the other two bacon slices, remaining tablespoon chives, and paprika oil. Serve at once.

CHOLON MODERN ASIAN BISTRO

1555 BLAKE STREET
DENVER, CO 80202
(303) 353-5223
CHOLON.COM
CHEF/CO-OWNER: LON SYMENSMA
CO-OWNERS: JIM DETERS AND ALICIA POKOIK DETERS

With all due respect to the Chairman of the Board, success in New York is not a safe predictor of career achievement beyond the boroughs; Coloradans have coolly waved off more than one big-name restaurateur in recent years. So why would Lon Symensma alter the trajectory of his own rising star—first at Jean-Georges Vongerichten's Spice Market, then Stephen Starr's Buddakan—and leave Manhattan to risk burnout in the Mile High City? Chalk it up to the pioneering spirit he shares with his adopted townspeople: "Denver's young, forward-thinking, and ready for what's coming."

Clearly, we were hungry for a place like ChoLon, given the dearth of upscale, contemporary Asian options in LoDo. Taking the name from a Chinese market in Vietnam (one that just so happens to echo his own), chef-partner Symensma immediately delivered in a space where minimalism takes on paradoxically opulent overtones. High ceilings, giant picture windows, and drum chandeliers fill the dining room with light, reflected by the marble floor tiles; running the length of one wall, the open kitchen gleams in white and silver; river stones and greenery line the dividers between the banquettes; and cool taupes and grays convey a serenity to counteract the steady buzz at peak hours (which acoustic panels help to absorb as well). The food naturally fits right in, deceptively simple and intricately presented from seasonal creations like celery-root soup with Asian pear and miso butterscotch to signatures such as the black-pepper short rib over fresh *chow fun* tossed with Chinese broccoli. (And dessert dim sum is a hoot, the seasonal assortment ranging from almond cookies and cashew brittle to green-tea macarons and passion-fruit jellies.)

Symensma credits extensive travels throughout Asia and Europe for the

development of his simultaneously painstaking and playful style. "When you actually go to, say, Bangkok and experience what the cuisine is all about, then you have context for being inspired by the ingredients around you. So as long as your technique is fundamentally sound, you just need a story to tell." Take the *kaya* toast, which he calls "a surprise hit": "That's one of my favorite dishes from Singapore, where they eat it in the mornings and afternoons. But it's so damn good that I just had to put it on every menu. Over there, you'll get a very soft egg, seasoned with a little soy sauce and tons of fresh-cracked white pepper; I've refined the process so it doesn't dribble down the front of your shirt so much. When we first opened, maybe I'd sell three or four a day; now it's as much as eighty on a busy night." Though the recipe Symensma uses at the restaurant involves nitrogen dispensers and *sous vide* machines, he's graciously simplified it here for the home cook.

Kaya Toast with Poached Eggs & Coconut Jam

Any leftover jam will keep in a refrigerated, sealed container for three days.

(SERVES 6)

For the coconut jam:

1 cup coconut milk
¾ cup sugar, divided
½ tablespoon salt
2 pandan leaves (available at Asian markets)
3 large eggs plus 3 yolks

For the eggs:

6 large eggs
1 tablespoon white vinegar
Cracked white pepper and soy sauce to taste

For the toast:

Softened butter as directed
6 slices good-quality white bread, 1¼ inches thick,
  crust removed

Special equipment:

double boiler (optional)
waterproof kitchen thermometer
6 small dipping bowls

To make the coconut jam, whisk together the coconut milk, half of the sugar (6 tablespoons), and salt in a large saucepan. Add the pandan leaves and bring to a boil. Shut off the heat and steep for 10 minutes. Remove leaves, squeeze them over the pan to extract as much liquid as possible, and discard. In a mixing bowl, combine the 3 whole eggs and 3 yolks with the remaining sugar and whisk until smooth; gradually whisk in the warm coconut milk. Transfer to a double boiler (or you can use a stainless-steel bowl that fits over the top of a saucepot) and cook, gently whisking constantly until the mixture thickens, about 20 minutes. Remove from heat and cool to room temperature, covering the surface of the jam directly with plastic wrap to avoid the formation of a skin.

Add enough water to cover the eggs you will be poaching to a small pot over medium heat, bring to 180°F (check with thermometer), and stir in vinegar. Gently crack 1 egg into a small glass bowl. Stir the water to form a gentle whirlpool and pour the egg into the center; cook for 2 minutes. Gently transfer to one of the six dipping bowls; repeat with the remaining eggs.

Butter the sliced bread on both sides and toast until golden brown. Slather one side of each slice with the coconut jam and place on a serving plate; repeat for the other 5 slices. Season the poached eggs generously with white pepper and soy sauce and serve alongside the toast for dipping.

COLT & GRAY

1553 PLATTE STREET
DENVER, CO 80202
(303) 477-1447
COLTANDGRAY.COM
CHEF/CO-OWNER: NELSON PERKINS
CO-OWNER: ALLISON PERKINS

Nelson Perkins is not one to flinch. From conception to ongoing expansion, the chef-owner's every move with respect to Colt & Gray has been deliberate and uncompromising—and the Platte River Valley destination is not only the better for it but one of the best in town.

Inspired by the UK gastropub movement, whose arrival stateside dovetailed so smoothly with our own craft-cocktail revival in the mid-aughts, Perkins (pictured left) elaborated on the model to create an environment that, admittedly, bespeaks some private club more than a public tavern, all creamy butterscotch leather and alligator trim against crisp whites and lacquered blacks. If "our first menu was a little more conservative" than it is today, the native son of cattle ranchers says, its evolution was no fluke: "I grew up in Colorado and had a pretty good idea of what Denver was going to accept in 2009. I used those early menus to gain people's trust—but serving offal was always part of the vision, and serving more game will be, too." Fearlessly inventive yet firmly grounded in European tradition, his repertoire today is rife with trotters and tongue, gizzards and glands, beautifully integrated into platters and plates that abound as well in seasonal farmhouse flourishes—escarole chutney, red *kuri* spaetzle, lavender glaze, and so on. Meanwhile, self-described "head barkeep" Kevin Burke (pictured right) has emerged as one of the city's most noted cocktailians, pouring drinks so gracefully composed they're almost choreographed (he is, after all, a professional dancer as well).

Renovation plans have long been in the works: The storefront adjacent to the bar should have been converted into a second dining room by the time this book is out, and the basement will house a USDA-approved meat-curing facility, a space for private functions, and a lounge called Ste. Ellie's, where Burke's already-underground craft-beer program will continue to lure "the geeks that can suck down a keg of some one-off special in a night," as Perkins laughs. So long as there's still room for us to swing by for a glass of sparkling rosé and a spot of head cheese come happy hour, everybody's bound to be happy.

Grass-Fed Beef Heart Tartare with Bread Soufflés, Diced Beets & Quail Egg Yolk

Contact your butcher in advance about obtaining cleaned organ meat from pasture-raised cows; quail eggs are usually available at Asian groceries. Both the consistency of the *tartare* and the intensity of its seasonings are up to you (the quantities listed below are standard but not fixed).

You will need several hours to prepare the soufflés; if there are some left over, you can store them in an airtight container for a day or so. Or, if preferred, you can serve the *tartare* with crostini instead.

(SERVES 4)

For the bread soufflés (inspired by Spanish chef Joan Roca):

2 cups high-gluten flour, plus extra as needed
2 cups low-gluten flour, plus extra as needed
1 scant tablespoon brewer's yeast
7 fluid ounces water, plus extra as needed
¼ teaspoon curry powder

For the beets:

1 large beet, rinsed and trimmed
1 tablespoon extra-virgin olive oil
1 teaspoon raspberry vinegar
Salt and freshly ground black pepper to taste

For the tartare:

1 pound cleaned, trimmed beef heart, finely minced or coarsely ground according to preference
1 tablespoon Dijon mustard
1 tablespoon mayonnaise
1 teaspoon high-quality extra-virgin olive oil (Perkins recommends Gianfranco Becchina Olio Verde)
2 teaspoons minced cornichons
2 teaspoons minced shallot
1½ teaspoons minced capers
¾ teaspoon minced garlic
Pinch of freshly ground star anise (grind in a mortar with pestle or in a spice/coffee mill)

Salt, freshly ground black pepper, and freshly squeezed lemon juice to taste
4 quail egg yolks
Piment d'Espelette to finish (paprika is an adequate substitute)

Special equipment:

pasta machine
hand-held pasta cutter
parchment paper
individual ring mold

Combine the flours in a mixing bowl to form a volcano shape. Dilute the yeast in the water and place the mixture with the curry powder into the center of the flour mound. Mix by hand, adding more combined flour and water as necessary to obtain a smooth, elastic dough (this should take 10–15 minutes). Wrap the dough tightly in plastic and refrigerate for a minimum of 6 hours.

While the dough is resting, make the beets: Preheat the oven to 375°F. Wrap the beet in aluminum foil and roast until tender, about 1½ hours. Remove and let cool; when ready to handle, peel and dice. Toss in olive oil and vinegar, season with salt and pepper, and set aside for at least 2 hours.

Increase the oven temperature to 450°F. Bring dough to room temperature for 30 minutes. Cut in pieces as necessary and then pass it through your pasta machine to create very fine sheets. Cut into ½-inch-wide strips with a pasta cutter; place on a baking sheet lined with parchment paper and bake about 10 minutes, watching carefully, until the dough rises and turns a light golden brown. Remove and let cool.

In a mixing bowl placed over a larger bowl filled with ice, gently combine all *tartare* ingredients except yolks and Espelette pepper, adjusting flavorings to taste. Store in the refrigerator if not using immediately (but for no longer than 1 hour).

Gently press 3–4 ounces *tartare* into your ring mold and carefully invert to release onto the center of one serving plate; repeat with three additional plates. Top each mound with the yolk of a quail egg and a sprinkle of Espelette pepper; add 3 or 4 soufflés (or crostini) and a tablespoon or so of diced beet per plate.

$400 Handcart

Infusing the bourbon will take about a week, and the results will keep for another two weeks—which gives you plenty of time to make three more cocktails just like this one! (The name is an allusion to the Mel Brooks classic *Blazing Saddles*—which "has spawned a number of different Manhattan-like cocktails," according to Burke.)

Though you don't have to use the brands of Bourbon and Sherry that Burke employs, he does suggest that the former have a spicy edge and that the latter be made in a sweet dessert style. Liquore Strega is a readily available Italian herbal liqueur; Scrappy's Original Lavender Bitters can be purchased online at scrappysbitters.com.

(SERVES 1)

8 fluid ounces (1 cup) bourbon (such as Buffalo Trace)
2 peach pits, cleaned of all fruit
1 wide lemon twist, cut with a vegetable peeler from a firm-skinned fruit
½ fluid ounce Pedro Ximénez Sherry (such as Alvear Solera 1927)
¼ fluid ounce Liquore Strega
3 drops Scrappy's Original Lavender Bitters
Luxardo or other high-end preserved cherry for garnish

To infuse the bourbon, preheat the oven to 450°F and roast the peach pits for 10 minutes. Cool and place in a clean glass jar with the bourbon; store for 1 week in a dry, dark place, shaking daily to agitate. Strain, discarding the pits, into a second clean glass container and store in the refrigerator.

Chill an old-fashioned glass. Express the oils of the lemon twist by pinching it at the center, pith side up, in a mixing glass; discard the peel. Add 2 fluid ounces infused bourbon (reserving the remainder for future use), Sherry, Strega, and ice; stir for 40 seconds to chill and dilute. Strain into the prepared glass over a large ice cube; add bitters and garnish with the cherry on a toothpick.

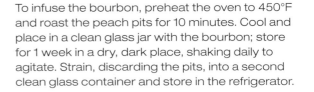

CURED

1825B PEARL STREET
BOULDER, CO 80304
(720) 389-8096
CUREDBOULDER.COM
OWNERS: WILL AND CORAL FRISCHKORN

Only in Boulder. Just a few doors down from the Berkeley of the Rockies' most celebrated dining destination, Frasca Food and Wine (page 68)—where master sommelier and marathon runner Bobby Stuckey holds court—sits Cured, a specialty grocery run by a former pro cyclist and his yogi wife. Catering as they do to a community founded, like few others, on the twin pillars of elite athleticism and connoisseurship, Will and Coral Frischkorn naturally stock the very stuff of the good life. Browsing every cranny of their sunny gourmet gallery can require the stamina of an art collector: At any given time, the shelves and display cases sparkle with packages of local honeycomb and bottles of imported anchovy extract, jars of duck fat and handmade chocolate truffles, rustic bread loaves and tins of flavored sea salt. With artisanal salumi and cheeses from as near as Durango and as far as Croatia. With exclusive *garagiste* microbrews and boutique spirits in the wine nook toward the back. If the sheer array exhausts you, an espresso from the in-store counter of Boxcar Coffee Roasters (303-527-1300; boxcarcoffeeroasters.com) should perk you right up—along with a sandwich built, enthuses Will, "around the very same products that we sell in the shop; we keep ingredient counts to a minimum and let the quality of the flavors speak for themselves."

That means the deviliciousness is in the details. For instance, though "any high-fat butter will do the trick, cheese-cultured Vermont butter adds that little extra something," according to Will. The preserves he prefers are made with Western Slope fruit and custom jarred for Cured by Colorado Mountain Jam. As for the ham, "we use a boiled French ham with high moisture and rich, amazing flavor." And finally, he adds, "If you have a panino press, by all means toss your sandwich on it to make a gourmet grilled cheese of sorts. The melting of flavors is delicious!"

THE FRENCH FIG

(SERVES 1)

⅓ long baguette

1 tablespoon unsalted butter, softened

3 ounces sliced boiled ham such as French *jambon blanc* or Italian *parmacotto*

1 tablespoon fig preserves

3 slices across the wheel of ripe brie, preferably Brie de Nangis

Slice the baguette lengthwise down the center. Spread one half with butter and top with loosely bunched slices of ham; spread the other half with preserves and add the cheese. Close the sandwich, wrap it, head outdoors with a bottle of rosé, and enjoy!

THE SPICY FRENCHMAN

(SERVES 1)

⅓ long baguette

1 tablespoon unsalted butter, softened

3 ounces sliced boiled ham such as French *jambon blanc* or Italian *parmacotto*

1 tablespoon peach-jalapeño or equivalent jam

3 slices across the wheel of ripe brie, preferably Brie de Nangis

Follow the instructions for the French Fig sandwich, replacing the fig preserves with the spicy peach jam.

ELWAY'S

2500 EAST 1ST AVENUE
DENVER, CO 80206
(303) 399-5353
ELWAYS.COM
OWNERS: JOHN ELWAY AND TIM SCHMIDT; CHEF: TYLER WIARD

In a funny way, the very fact Elway's had so much going for it from day one could have been a big black mark against it. As a steak house emblazoned with the signature of a legendary Broncos quarterback, it would certainly enjoy a built-in following: After all, Denver was still very much a beef-and-potatoes town when it opened in 2004—the same year its namesake was inducted into the Pro Football Hall of Fame. And then there was the matter of its location, location, location—right in the backyard of its obvious target

market, the well-heeled denizens of Cherry Creek North. Talk about throwing red meat to your audience. But given that conspicuous consumption comes with the territory, Elway's appeal might easily have been lost on those gastronomes for whom inspired cuisine trumps celebrity glitz.

That it isn't is all to the credit of chef Tyler Wiard, whose serious chops (no pun intended) inform a menu that sincerely honors without paying slavish deference to cow-palace standards. Sure, hand-cut prime steaks and fresh seafood form its luxurious core: Think hefty bone-in rib eyes and New York strips, lobster tails and shellfish towers, along with traditional à la carte sides like twice-baked potatoes and creamed spinach. But as Wiard tells his staff, "If you guys can continue to make the quote 'old stuff' perfect every time, then we can play." And play they do, turning out seasonal winners like roast halibut with quinoa, edamame, preserved lemon, and a drizzle of *giardiniera* vinaigrette; pistachio-studded brussels sprout hash; and jaw-dropping chicken-fried steak burritos smothered in sausage gravy for brunch.

Still, the setting is unabashedly paradigmatic. To one side of the marble fountain marking the entrance, warm woods and sandstone hues lend the stately dining room a Southwestern glow. To the other side—flanked by a covered wraparound patio and lined with cases displaying Elway's jerseys and helmets—is a piano bar whose

reputation as a business-class singles scene rather comically precedes it. In short, the flagship of what you could now call a mini-franchise yields a true Colorado experience through and through. (There's also an outpost in The Ritz-Carlton Denver at 1881 Curtis Street, 303-312-3826; one at Denver International Airport, Concourse B; and a third in Vail.)

Lamb Fondue

If you're not a fan of lamb (perish the thought), this fondue also works well with tortilla chips. Elway's Seasoning can be purchased via the restaurant website.

(SERVES 8–10)

For the green chile–cheese fondue:

1 whole Anaheim chile

2 whole serrano chiles

2 whole poblano chiles

2 tablespoons unsalted butter

¼ cup peeled and julienned yellow onion

½ teaspoon salt, plus extra to taste

1 tablespoon chopped fresh garlic, smashed to a paste

1–1½ ounces *tequila plata* (silver tequila)

1 cup heavy cream

1 cup half-and-half

½ cup grated Pepper Jack cheese

½ cup grated muenster cheese

½ cup grated white cheddar

Elway's Seasoning (or substitute salt and pepper)

30 lamb rib chops

Special equipment:

stick blender (optional)

outdoor grill

Directly over the flame of a gas burner or under a hot broiler, roast all chiles, turning as necessary, until the skins are completely blackened. Let cool, then remove charred skins, stems, and ribs and chop the chiles roughly, retaining seeds.

In a heavy saucepan, melt butter completely; add onion and ½ teaspoon salt. Cook 5–10 minutes, stirring frequently, until onion is translucent. Add garlic; cook for another 2–3 minutes, then deglaze with tequila. Add chiles to the onion mixture and stir to combine; add cream and half-and-half. Cook until liquids have reduced by one-third, approximately 10–15 minutes.

With a stick blender (you may use a whisk if necessary), incorporate cheeses a handful at a time, making sure that each is fully melted and smooth before adding the next. After all the cheese is fully incorporated, season with salt to taste and check for consistency—it should be hollandaise-like. Keep warm.

Prepare grill. Season lamb chops evenly on all sides and grill to medium-rare, about 4–5 minutes per side. Serve on a platter with a large bowl of fondue.

Euclid Hall Bar & Kitchen

1317 14th Street
Denver, CO 80202
(303) 595-4255
euclidhall.com
Chef/Co-Owner: Jennifer Jasinski; Co-Owner: Beth Gruitch
Chef de Cuisine: Jorel Pierce

The history here is ingrained. Though the nineteenth-century double-decker that now houses this rollicking LoDo gastropub has been stripped down to the bare mod-industrial elements—exposed brick, black metal, planked wood—there's still something in the air that speaks to its bygone days as a doctor's manor, the headquarters of the Woman's Relief Corps, a Masonic lodge . . . and, reputedly, a brothel.

Maybe it's just the echoes of conversation and laughter bouncing off all those hard surfaces, heard but only half-understood, not unlike the past itself. Or maybe it's the old-timey moustaches and newsboy gear sported by some of the dapper gents on staff. Certainly, the food plays no small role in the retro mood: Partner Jennifer Jasinski and chef de cuisine Jorel Pierce (pictured), along with pastry chef Eric Dale, have crafted a menu that hearkens back by turns to Old World *biergartens,* New England's clam shacks, the delicatessens of the Lower East Side, even heartland county fairs.

Which isn't to say it clings to convention. On the contrary, for this crew, nostalgia is merely a backdrop against which to construct grand displays of cross-cultural moxie. The mess of french fries, cheese curds, and gravy that is Québécois *poutine* here gains a Mexican complexion with tomatillos, green chiles, cilantro, and lime. Via the application of haute technique to soul food's biggest sleeper hit, fried chicken and waffles come doused in black pepper béchamel and maple gastrique. A childhood novelty treat returns

as chocolate-covered-popcorn ice cream in a waffle cone. And pad thai pig ears have the makings of a culinary icon.

Meanwhile the beer list is unabashedly geeky, categorized by style under mathematical headings in honor of Euclid himself: "Arithmetic" covers sessionable lagers, "Calculus" bigger and more complex ales, and so on. As a result, the next chapter in the folklore of Euclid Hall is now being written by the craft-brew connoisseurs who descend on Denver each fall to attend the Great American Beer Festival—and to make the rounds of suds hubs like this one after hours, savoring rare find after rare find. If only these walls really could talk . . . well, they'd probably slur their words. But we'd know what they meant.

HOUSE PICKLES

Though billed as an à la carte condiment, Euclid Hall's house-pickle sampler makes for a fine snack in and of itself.

PICKLING SPICE BLEND
(MAKES 1 CUP)

4 tablespoons coriander seed

3 tablespoons black peppercorns

2¾ tablespoons mustard seed

2½ tablespoons allspice

2¼ tablespoons red pepper flakes

1½ tablespoons mace

1½ tablespoons ground ginger

1 tablespoon whole cloves

1 cinnamon stick, crushed into small pieces

18 bay leaves

Combine all ingredients thoroughly and store in a tightly lidded glass or plastic container in a cool, dry, dark place. You can pickle a variety of vegetables with this mixture, including cauliflower, carrots, and green beans.

DILL PICKLES
(MAKES ABOUT 30 PICKLES)

2¾ tablespoons Pickling Spice Blend

1½ gallons water

¾ cup Champagne vinegar

⅓ cup kosher salt

¾ tablespoon black peppercorns

¾ tablespoon dill seed

2 ounces fresh dill (about 1 loosely packed cup—stems okay)

4 pounds blemish-free pickling cucumbers of uniform size

Special equipment:

2 (1-gallon) glass containers with tight-fitting lids

Combine all ingredients except fresh dill and cucumbers in a large pot and bring to a boil; reduce heat and simmer for 3 minutes. Cool to room temperature.

Divide dill and cucumbers evenly between two 1-gallon containers and pour in brine to cover, allowing at least a 1-inch gap of headspace. Insert a small dish made of glass, porcelain, or plastic on top of the pickles to keep them from bobbing up above the brining solution. (Do not use any type of metal, which can cause discoloration and softening.) Tightly seal containers, place in the refrigerator, and brine for 10 days before using.

Hoppy Pickles

(MAKES ABOUT 30 PICKLES)

2¾ tablespoons Pickling Spice Blend

1½ gallons water

¾ cup Champagne vinegar

⅓ cup kosher salt

2¼ tablespoons hot pepper flakes

¾ tablespoon black peppercorns

¾ tablespoon dill seed

3 ounces high alpha acid hops, such as Centennial or Cascade (available at home-brewing supply shops)

4 pounds blemish-free pickling cucumbers of uniform size

Special equipment:

2 (1-gallon) glass containers with tight-fitting lids

Combine all ingredients except cucumbers in a large pot and bring to a boil; reduce heat and simmer for 3 minutes. Cool to room temperature.

Divide cucumbers evenly between two 1-gallon containers and pour in brine to cover, allowing at least a 1-inch gap of headspace. Insert a small dish made of glass, porcelain, or plastic on top of the pickles to keep them from bobbing up above the brining solution. (Do not use any type of metal, which can cause discoloration and softening.) Tightly seal containers, place in the refrigerator, and brine for 10 days before using.

Spicy Pickles

(MAKES ABOUT 30 PICKLES)

2½ tablespoons Pickling Spice Blend

1½ gallons water

¾ cup Champagne vinegar

⅓ cup kosher salt

¾ ounce serrano chiles, destemmed, deseeded, and halved lengthwise

¼ ounce *chile de arbol,* destemmed, deseeded, and toasted in a small pan over medium-high heat until fragrant and somewhat softened

1 tablespoon black peppercorns

1 tablespoon dill seed

2 ounces fresh dill (about 1 loosely packed cup—stems okay)

4 pounds blemish-free pickling cucumbers of uniform size

Special equipment:

2 (1-gallon) glass containers with tight-fitting lids

Combine all ingredients except fresh dill and cucumbers in a large pot and bring to a boil; reduce heat and simmer for 3 minutes. Cool to room temperature.

Divide dill and cucumbers evenly between two 1-gallon containers and pour in brine to cover, allowing at least a 1-inch gap of headspace. Insert a small dish made of glass, porcelain, or plastic on top of the pickles to keep them from bobbing up above the brining solution. (Do not use any type of metal, which can cause discoloration and softening.) Tightly seal containers, place in the refrigerator, and brine for 10 days before using.

FLAGSTAFF HOUSE

1138 FLAGSTAFF ROAD
BOULDER, CO 80302
(303) 442-4640
FLAGSTAFFHOUSE.COM
CHEF/CO-OWNER: MARK MONETTE
CO-OWNERS: SCOTT AND DON MONETTE

Though it's historically accurate, the phrase "Depression-era mountain cabin" doesn't begin to describe what the Flagstaff House has become over the course of its eighty-year existence, especially since the Monette family purchased it in 1971. "Glass-walled, terrace-lined, peak-side shrine to fine wining and dining" is more like it.

Not a celebratory detail goes overlooked here. Tables set with white linens and crystal glitter like the Boulder skyline they overlook. From the first *amuse bouche* to the last sweetmeat, the service is as crisp as the uniforms of a staff who can walk you, via the iPad list, through a world-class wine cellar that houses upward of three thousand selections; if you've ever dreamed of trading in your nest egg for a vertical tasting of

Château Mouton-Rothschild, now's your chance. And then there's the menu, swathed in luxuries the way some of your fellow patrons are sure to be dripping in diamonds: truffles, caviar, quail, soft-shell crab, lobster, and the ever-obligatory foie gras.

Which isn't to suggest it's merely a tool for conspicuous consumption. Having trained all over the world, chef Mark Monette returned in 1985 to the kitchen where he started as a teen, and he's been refining his oeuvre ever since to include the likes of, say, braised Kurobuta pork belly with bourbon-peach coulis on french toast or a duo of sesame-crusted ahi tuna and coconut-crusted oysters alongside warm cucumber-seaweed salad, followed perhaps by a dish of white pepper–goat cheese ice cream and an assortment of locally made truffles. To him, this is practically home cooking. To those of us who didn't grow up in the back of one of Colorado's foremost houses, it's something incredibly special.

LOBSTER SOUP WITH RICE & SHIITAKES

Lobster lovers who save their shells for stock might try this recipe for their next dinner party instead.

(SERVES 8–10)

Shells from 10 pounds lobster bodies
1 cup plus 1 dash brandy
2 cups white wine
2 carrots, chopped
2 celery stalks, chopped
2 yellow onions, chopped
1 bunch leeks, green part only, chopped
½ garlic bulb, unpeeled
½ cup uncooked white rice
1 gallon fish stock
1 cup tomato paste
8–10 black peppercorns
1 sprig thyme
4 bay leaves
1 quart heavy whipping cream
2 tablespoons butter, softened
Salt, white pepper, and cayenne pepper to taste
8–10 thinly sliced shiitake mushrooms

Preheat the oven to 400°F.

Place lobster shells in a very large, ovenproof pot and roast in the oven until brown or dry, 20–30 minutes. Remove from the oven and place on the stove over medium heat. Deglaze with 1 cup brandy and white wine; add carrots, celery, onions, leeks, garlic, and rice. Cover with fish stock; stir in tomato paste, peppercorns, thyme, and bay leaves; and bring to a simmer. Cook for 1 hour.

With a fine-mesh sieve, carefully transfer all the solids in the pot to a food processor and puree (in batches as necessary). Strain the puree back into the pot, discarding the pulp, and return to a simmer.

In another pot over medium heat, reduce cream by one-third (this should take 10–15 minutes), then stir it slowly into the soup. Simmer for 15 minutes. Stir in the butter, add a dash of brandy, season to taste, and serve in bowls topped with sliced shiitakes.

FRASCA FOOD AND WINE

1738 PEARL STREET
BOULDER, CO 80302
(303) 442-6966
FRASCAFOODANDWINE.COM
CHEF/CO-OWNER: LACHLAN MACKINNON-PATTERSON
CO-OWNER: BOBBY STUCKEY

In hindsight, it's easy to declare that Boulder's, if not Colorado's, preeminent dining destination would achieve greatness upon opening its doors in 2004. After all, the combined résumé of chef-owner Lachlan Mackinnon-Patterson and his partner, master sommelier Bobby Stuckey, included stints at Michelin-starred restaurants in France, The Little Nell in Aspen, and The French Laundry; scrappy upstarts these guys were not.

But whether their adopted college town would readily grasp the concept of Friulian cuisine could only have been anybody's guess. Even today, the northeastern Italian region that serves as their primary inspiration isn't well known stateside; the duo was

taking a real chance on nigh-unpronounceable dishes and obscure wines made from a dizzying array of indigenous grapes.

It paid off in spades—as the receipt of more than one James Beard Foundation Award attests. Mackinnon-Patterson continues to turn out creations of uncommon warmth and grace: Rest assured that if you've never heard of *calamarata* (a pasta shaped, as the name suggests, like squid rings) or *nduja* (a soft, spicy pork sausage) or couscous-like *fregola,* you won't forget it once you've tried it here, incorporated in ways that radiate a sense of place and season. The same goes for a bottle of Malvasia Istriana or Schioppettino from a cellar that may well, in its collection of rare regional treasures, be unmatched anywhere—Italy included.

Or rather, don't take it from us—let the tremendous staff do all the reassuring. Whatever they may do in their off-hours, they live and breathe hospitality on the floor; there's not an ingredient they can't elucidate, not a request they can't field. By meal's end, you feel not only satisfied in body and cared for in spirit but even stimulated in mind. It is a capital-*e* Experience.

Chestnut Soup

From Thanksgiving through New Year's Eve, chestnuts are everywhere; you'll find them both preroasted in the jar or stored loose and fresh. Beyond the holiday season, you should be able to purchase them online. If you opt to cook them yourself, we find the easiest method to be broiling: Preheat your broiler, slice off the chestnuts' oval tops, cook for 20 to 30 minutes (turning once), and slip off the skins with a dish towel. But a quick search online will yield countless alternatives for boiling or roasting them.

(SERVES 4 AS AN APPETIZER)

1 tablespoon butter

¼ cup chopped yellow onion

1 ounce minced prosciutto or speck

½ teaspoon salt

3 tablespoons peeled, chopped Honey Crisp apple

About 9 ounces (or 2 cups) cooked, peeled, chopped chestnuts, divided

3 cups water

3 tablespoons heavy whipping cream

4 teaspoons crème frâiche

4 teaspoons minced chives

Special equipment:

chinois or other fine-mesh strainer

In a medium-size saucepan over medium-high heat, melt butter and cook onion and prosciutto (or speck) a few minutes until translucent. Add salt, apple, and all but 4 teaspoons chestnuts; toss to coat in the fat. Add water and cream and simmer for 20 minutes.

Transfer the soup to a food processor and blend. Strain through a chinois and serve in four small bowls with a teaspoon each of crème frâiche, chives, and reserved chestnuts.

Frangipane Pear Tart

Frangipane is an almond-flavored pastry filling, often containing nut paste but in this case made with flour. For precise measurements in grams, use of a digital scale is recommended.

(MAKES 1 TART)

For the pears:

600 grams sugar
200 milliliters white wine
Ice cubes made from 1 liter water
4 ripe (but not overripe) Bartlett pears, carefully peeled

For the crust:

81.25 grams butter, at room temperature
68.75 grams confectioners' sugar
62.5 grams egg yolk
187.5 grams all-purpose flour, plus extra as directed
3.75 grams salt

For the pastry cream:

115 grams half-and-half
¼ vanilla bean
18 grams sugar, divided
22 grams egg yolk
3.8 grams cornstarch
11 grams butter, softened

For the frangipane:

100 grams butter, softened
100 grams sugar
30 grams egg yolk
100 grams almond flour
20 grams all-purpose flour
1 gram salt
75 grams egg white

For the garnish:

¼ cup smooth apricot preserves, melted over low heat in a small saucepan with 1 tablespoon water

Special equipment:

digital scale
hand mixer (optional)
10-inch pie pan
chinois
melon baller
pastry brush

First, poach the pears: In a good-size nonreactive pot, bring the sugar and white wine to a boil, then add the ice and turn off the heat. When cool, submerge the pears in the poaching liquid and cook at a low simmer until fork-tender (15–30 minutes, depending on the size of the fruit). Set pot aside to cool, leaving the pears in the liquid.

Next, prepare the tart shell: In a food processor or with a hand mixer, cream butter and sugar just until sugar is incorporated. Add yolk and combine, scraping the bowl with a spatula as you go. Add 187.5 grams flour and salt; mix until integrated.

Place dough on a clean work surface and sprinkle it with more flour, turning as you go, until it is no longer sticky. Shape into a crust inside your pie pan.

To make the pastry cream: Add half-and-half, vanilla bean, and 9 grams sugar to a small saucepan and scald (that is, heat to just below the boiling point) over medium heat. In a bowl, whisk

egg yolk, remaining sugar, and cornstarch until smooth. Temper the yolk mixture by whisking in small amounts of the scalded liquid and add it to the saucepan; whisk constantly until the pastry cream has come to a boil and thickened (about 10 minutes). Taste to ensure that all the cornstarch has cooked out, then strain into a bowl through a chinois and whisk in the butter. In a larger bowl, prepare an ice bath; place the pastry-cream bowl in the ice and let it cool, stirring often. After about 20 minutes, the texture will be smooth.

To start the frangipane: Cream butter and sugar as before; add yolk slowly until combined, then mix in the flours and salt well. Add the pastry cream until combined. Cover and chill in the freezer for 20 minutes or until cold.

Preheat the oven to 325°F. Dock the tart shell by pricking it in several places with a fork, then bake for 10 minutes; reduce heat to 280°F and continue to bake, rotating every 7–8 minutes until a golden color is achieved. This will take about 20 minutes.

Meanwhile, remove the pears from the poaching liquid and halve them lengthwise. Carefully remove the cores with a melon baller and cut into slices ¼-inch thick. To finish the frangipane, whip egg whites in a bowl with a whisk or hand mixer until they form soft peaks, then fold into the chilled base.

When the tart shell is ready, increase the oven temperature to 350°F. Spread the frangipane evenly on the bottom of the shell. Beginning at the center of the tart, lay the sliced pears atop the frangipane in rows that radiate outward from the center toward the edge, each slice overlapping the last.

Bake the tart, giving it a turn every 10 minutes to assure even caramelization. When it is deeply golden (30–40 minutes), remove and let cool. Just before serving, brush the surface with a glaze of apricot preserves.

FRUITION RESTAURANT

1313 EAST 6TH AVENUE
DENVER, CO 80203
(303) 831-1962
FRUITIONRESTAURANT.COM
CHEF/OWNER: ALEX SEIDEL; CHEF DE CUISINE: MATTHEW VAWTER

Like everything else about this slice of European farmhouse life in the Country Club neighborhood, the name is an understatement. Set in an old converted row house, the small, candlelit dining room invites you to dwell in simplicity: Bare tables, wood floors, and scattered artwork keep distractions to a minimum—all the better for concentrating on the subtleties of the seasonal cuisine. Over six years and counting, Alex Seidel's studious efforts both in the kitchen and on his combination ranch, creamery, and greenhouse in Larkspur have indeed come to fruition, yielding national acclaim and local adoration.

"From the moment we opened to this day, I've always wanted people to feel as comfortable as if they were coming to a dinner party at my house," Seidel (pictured left) says. Generating that level of trust is a staff of seasoned long-timers who know the menu and beverage selection inside and out, down to the details of the homegrown

ingredients. Precision (but not fussiness) is the hallmark of a kitchen whose output is as intricate as it is surprisingly earthy: rabbit braised in red wine and served over cauliflower ravioli and conserved mushrooms in truffled jus, say, or pork-shoulder schnitzel with spaetzle, winter squash, caramelized brussels sprouts, and Riesling-apple butter, followed by the signature lemon-meringue pie with blueberry compote. The wine list is likewise serious but not stuffy, the array of bottled craft beers remarkable for an operation of this size (especially when it comes to Belgian styles)—and the after-dinner offerings delightfully deep, from Austrian Trockenbeernenauslese to copious Cognacs.

Asked about Fruition's place in the Denver dining scene, Seidel humbly defers to "the people around us. I don't think it's up to us to make that judgment." Fair enough—we submit that it's front and center.

Fruition Farms Shepherd's Halo with Semolina Zeppole, Tomato Marmalade, Olive Oil Jam & Pickled Red Onion Salad

Zeppole are essentially Italian doughnut holes, which may be savory or sweet. Though they're bound to go fast, you'll have more pickled onions and tomato marmalade than you need for this recipe; both will keep, stored in the refrigerator, for about a week. The former would also be great on sandwiches; as for the jam, says chef de cuisine Matt Vawter (pictured right), just thin it out with some olive oil and vinegar, toss in a little chopped shallot, and *voilà!*—you've got a zesty salad dressing.

Many local, independent cheesemongers carry Fruition Farms products.

(SERVES 8)

For the pickled onions:

1 cup white wine vinegar
¼ cup red wine
¼ cup sugar
1 bay leaf
1 teaspoon crushed coriander seed
1 teaspoon white peppercorn
1 teaspoon mustard seed
2 red onions

For the tomato marmalade:

6 ripe, seasonal tomatoes of different colors
1 cup red wine vinegar
½ cup sugar
1 teaspoon salt, plus extra to taste

For the olive oil jam:

Scant ⅓ cup light corn syrup
3 egg yolks
1½ teaspoons kosher salt
1 cup plus 2 tablespoons olive oil

For the zeppole:

4–5 cups peanut, grapeseed, or canola oil
   (this should be sufficient, but have some extra
   at the ready)
1 egg
½ cup sugar
2 teaspoons melted unsalted butter
½ cup milk
1 cup flour
¼ cup semolina flour
1½ teaspoons baking powder
¼ teaspoon salt
Confectioners' sugar for dusting

18 sprigs frisée, cleaned and dried
1 wheel Fruition Farms Shepherd's Halo, cut into
   8 wedges and brought to room temperature
   (or use about 12 ounces of any soft, ripened
   sheep's milk cheese)
Aged balsamic vinegar to drizzle

Special equipment:

deep-fat fryer and/or frying thermometer

To make the pickled onions: Bring all ingredients except onions to a boil in a medium pot; then shut off the heat and steep 1 hour. Meanwhile, peel and slice onions thinly into rings and place in a stainless-steel or glass bowl. When the marinade is ready, strain to remove solids and pour the remaining liquid over the onions. Cover bowl and cool in refrigerator at least 4 hours and up to a week in advance.

To make the marmalade: Prepare an ice bath in a large bowl and bring a large pot of water to a boil over high heat. Remove the core from the top of each tomato and cut a small X on the bottom. Blanch in boiling water for 15 seconds and shock in ice bath; then remove the skins (they should peel easily), cut the tomatoes in half laterally, and scoop out the seeds. Roughly chop the remaining flesh.

Place the vinegar, sugar, and 1 teaspoon salt in a good-size pot and bring to a boil on the stovetop. Add chopped tomatoes, reduce heat to a simmer, and cook until the liquid has nearly evaporated and the pot is almost dry. Remove from the heat and season to taste with salt, then transfer to a glass or plastic bowl and cool to room temperature.

To prepare the olive oil jam: Place the corn syrup in a pot and bring to a boil on the stovetop. Meanwhile, whip egg yolks in a food processor. With motor running, add boiling syrup in a steady but careful stream—if the mixture gets too hot, it will break. Add salt, and then add the olive oil slowly to emulsify; when it looks like translucent mayonnaise, set aside in a glass bowl.

To make the *zeppole:* Start by heating the oil in a deep-fat fryer or good-size pot over high heat until it reaches 350°F. Next, whisk egg and sugar together in a bowl until combined. Add melted butter and milk; sift in the dry ingredients (except confectioners' sugar) and whisk to incorporate until you're left with a thick batter. With a spoon or ice-cream scoop, gently drop balls of batter into the oil in batches (don't overcrowd) and cook until golden brown, about 2 minutes; depending on batch size, you may need to add more oil. Remove to a surface covered with paper towels to drain; then place an equal amount of the fried *zeppole* on eight serving plates and dust with confectioners' sugar.

In a separate bowl, toss the frisée with some pickled onions; top the *zeppole* with a small mound of salad and finish each plate with a wedge of cheese, a *quenelle* (oval-shaped dollop) of tomato marmalade, and another of olive oil jam. Garnish with a drizzle of balsamic vinegar.

Heirloom Tomato-and-Fried Eggplant Salad with Roasted Eggplant Hummus, Fruition Farms Ricotta & Toasted Pine Nut Emulsion

Roast the head of garlic in advance: Cut off the top of the head so the clove tips are exposed, drizzle in a little olive oil, wrap the head in foil, and bake in a 275°F oven until soft (at least 1 hour).

(SERVES 8)

For the hummus:

2 medium Italian eggplants
Canola oil for rubbing
Salt as directed
Pepper to taste
2 cups canned chickpeas
Cloves from 1 head roasted garlic
1 teaspoon tahini paste
Juice of 1 lemon
3 tablespoons extra-virgin olive oil

For the pine nut emulsion:

1 cup pine nuts
2 tablespoons balsamic vinegar
Water as needed
Salt to taste

For the vinaigrette:

1 shallot, minced
¼ cup red wine vinegar
¾ cup canola oil
2 teaspoons salt, plus extra to taste
1 teaspoon ground white pepper, plus extra to taste

For the fried eggplant:

Peanut, grapeseed, or canola oil as directed
1 large Chinese eggplant
1 cup all-purpose flour
5 eggs, whisked to combine
1 cup panko bread crumbs

¼ cup pine nuts
8 heirloom tomatoes of different colors, blanched and
    peeled (see previous recipe for instructions)
Salt and black pepper to taste
1 cup Fruition Farms (or other fresh) ricotta
Micro-arugula for garnish (optional)

Special equipment:

deep-fat fryer and/or frying thermometer
offset spatula
pastry bag and small, straight tip

Preheat the oven to 400°F.

To make the hummus: Begin by roasting the eggplants. Rub the skins with a little canola oil, sprinkle with salt and pepper, and roast in oven until tender, about 40 minutes. Halve lengthwise, scoop out the flesh (discarding the skins), and place it, along with 2 teaspoons salt and all remaining ingredients except olive oil, in a food processor. Puree until combined; then, while motor is running, slowly add olive oil to emulsify. Adjust salt to taste and set aside.

To make the pine nut emulsion: In a medium pan over medium-low heat, toast pine nuts, being careful not to burn them. Remove and let cool, then place in a blender, add balsamic vinegar, and begin to blend, adding water as needed to adjust the consistency; the finished product should be smooth and thick, like soft butter. Season with salt to taste and set aside.

To make the vinaigrette: Combine all ingredients in a mixing bowl and whisk to emulsify. Adjust seasoning as necessary and set aside.

Next, prepare the fried eggplant: Add 5 cups oil to a deep-fat fryer or enough to cover the bottom of a large, high-sided pan over high heat; bring to 350°F. Slice the eggplant into rounds. Place flour, whisked eggs, and panko crumbs in three separate bowls. One by one, dredge eggplant slices in flour, shaking off the excess; dip to coat in the egg; and dredge again in the bread crumbs. Fry the breaded slices, in batches as necessary so as not to overcrowd, about 2 minutes or until golden brown. Remove slices to surface covered with paper towels to drain.

To complete the recipe, toast ¼ cup pine nuts as before. Cut blanched tomatoes into five or six wedges each, depending on size. Place in a mixing bowl with nuts. Season with salt and pepper, then toss with vinaigrette.

On eight serving plates (preferably square if available), use an offset spatula to spread a thin layer of hummus on the base of the plate and wipe the edges clean. Lay four or five tomato wedges, alternating colors, from one corner of each plate to the opposite corner, making sure the pine nuts are evenly distributed. (There may be some tomato left over.) Using a pastry bag fitted with a small, straight tip, pipe the pine nut emulsion into the open spaces between the wedges. Place two crispy eggplant slices per plate on top of the wedges. Finish each plate with three *quenelles* of fresh ricotta; if you have access to micro-arugula, place a few sprigs around and atop the salad.

Green Russell

1422 Larimer Street
Denver, CO 80202
(303) 893-6505
greenrussell.com
Owners: Frank Bonanno and Adam Hodak

It took a few years for the revival of Prohibition-era cocktail culture to spread from the coasts inland—but Coloradans made up for lost time in a jiffy. After all, here at the forefront of microbrewing, a leap to craft distilling and bartending was only natural—and effortlessly made by local producers of spirits and liqueurs as well as the young guns (and gunettes) who dispense them.

Among the first on the scene was indefatigable chef-restaurateur Frank Bonanno and beverage director Adam Hodak (pictured), who kept their shared vision for an unmarked, subterranean lounge on Larimer Square that channeled the spirit of speakeasies past under wraps via the front of Wednesday's Pie (wednesdayspie.com). To this day, the checkerboard-tiled hole-in-the-wall (or rather hole-in-the-ground-floor) serves up pies by the slice while doubling as the foyer to Green Russell—every inch a return to another time and place. Gas lanterns flicker on rock walls and iron grates; gilt-edged mirrors and copper ceiling tiles cast a diffuse glow among the brass-studded black- and red-leather armchairs and barstools; a vintage phone booth stands in back for patrons otherwise dissuaded from breaking the mood through cell-phone usage. And you'd better believe the dandies behind the bar rise to the occasion of the setting.

As a matter of course, they make their own bitters, syrups, and sodas, many infused with herbs from the on-site grow room—which, says Hodak, also contains "a banana plant that could grow six feet in a year!" They do their own juicing and chip their own ice to fit the glass at hand. They experiment with barrel aging and recipes of old as they "look for ways to connect the past and present." About all they don't do? "Serve Jack and Coke," admits Hodak wryly. Instead, they encourage their customers to try "something they can't have for

three dollars at any dive," be it a seasonally appropriate concoction from the ever-changing menu or the "bartender's choice," customized impromptu to yield, perhaps, rye blended with chocolate-chipotle bitters, chamomile, and cinnamon-honey liqueur.

In 2011, Bonanno expanded his little underground warren to include barbecue joint Russell's Smokehouse (720-524-8050; russellssmokehouse.com), which means you can pair your poison with the likes of brisket sliders, pigs in a blanket made with pork belly and puff pastry—and, obviously, pie. But whatever you do, you can hardly go wrong here—short of demanding a round of Alabama Slammers while taking a call, that is.

CENTRAL PARK

Most craft bars tossed their stash of mass-produced, neon-red maraschino cherries years ago in favor of their gourmet equivalent; look for Italian imports like Amarena or Luxardo.

Leopold Bros. is a local distillery; its products are readily available at area retailers. Look for Regans' online.

(SERVES 1)

2 fluid ounces Leopold Bros. Rye Whiskey
1 fluid ounce Punt e Mes Sweet Vermouth
2 dashes Regans' Orange Bitters
6 medium-size basil leaves
2 strips lemon zest
4–6 lavender flowers, fresh or dried
Preserved cherry or orange zest for garnish

In mixing glass, stir all ingredients (except garnish) with ice until well chilled and properly diluted. Strain through fine-mesh sieve into a cocktail glass and garnish as desired with a cherry or orange zest.

THE INVENTING ROOM

(303) 885-2802
INVENTING-ROOM.COM
CHEF/OWNER: IAN KLEINMAN

Don't let Ian Kleinman hear you say "molecular gastronomy." He prefers the term "food entertainment" for the experimental cookery on which he's built quite the reputation. Having grown up in the industry—the Breckenridge native began work as a prep cook in his parents' restaurant, The Gold Pan, at age eleven—"I was getting bored with the day to day and was searching for a way to bring my passion back to cooking," he says. "I've always been fascinated with science, and when I found out I could combine the two, it was a no-brainer."

Well, a no-brainer for him, anyway. For the lucky attendees of events catered by his company, The Inventing Room, Kleinman's creations are—like those of the namesake laboratory in *Willy Wonka & the Chocolate Factory*—positively mind-bending. Imagine Moroccan-spiced chocolate truffles that, thanks to the use of magnets, float in midair. Think dates in the form of bubbles, coconut cubes, caper-flavored paper, and powdered bacon. Or consider his most "outrageous project," whereby "I made it snow flavors— guests walked in the room, turned their heads up with their mouths open, and tasted raspberry 'snow' falling from the ceiling."

Of course, such fun with chemistry requires a solid foundation in classical cooking technique. Like his father—who taught cooking in Oslo, Norway—before him, Kleinman's

dad was a culinary instructor at The Art Institute of Colorado, where Kleinman himself studied, concentrating on chocolate and sugar work; he went on to helm a number of kitchens and served as executive chef of the now-closed O's Restaurant in Westminster before striking out solo. A brick-and-mortar eatery is in the works, though the details were under wraps at press time; until it opens, you'll find this mad scientist working his magic at pop-ups and festivals throughout Denver—whipping up the likes of "*pho* pipettes," peanut butter–marshmallow doughnuts with "grape caviar," and "grilled margaritas with jalapeño foam." Hard to believe, easy to relish.

SHAVED VEGETABLES WITH SMOKED OLIVE OIL, GOAT CHEESE MARBLES & TOASTED PECANS

(SERVES 6)

8 fluid ounces (1 cup) olive oil, plus additional as directed

1 large red beet, well rinsed and trimmed

Salt and pepper as required

1 fennel bulb, with fronds

2 zucchini, cleaned and trimmed

2 yellow squash, cleaned and trimmed

2 carrots, trimmed and peeled

Juice of 1 lemon

5 ounces goat cheese

20 Korean red-pepper threads (available at specialty spice shops)

2 ounces (½ cup) coarsely chopped pecans, lightly toasted in a hot dry pan

Special equipment:

outdoor wood smoker, preferably using cherrywood or cedar smoking chips (optional)

Add oil to a large baking pan and place in smoker. Burn the chips for 10 minutes, then shut off (if electric) or remove heat source (if charcoal) and let the olive oil sit for 1 hour. Remove and reserve. (If you don't have a smoker, this can also be done over low heat on the stovetop; place the pan, covered with foil, directly on the burner.)

Preheat the oven to 350°F. Place the beet in a bowl and toss with pinches of salt and pepper and a little olive oil. Roast in oven for 1 hour or until fork-tender. Remove and set aside to cool; when ready to handle, cut the beet into twelve wedges.

Cut the top fronds off the fennel bulb, reserving 20 small sprigs, and trim the bottom of the bulb; slice fennel lengthwise into very thin strips and place in a bowl. Using a peeler, shave the zucchini, yellow squash, and carrots lengthwise and add to the fennel. Toss the shaved vegetables with ¼ cup smoked olive oil and lemon juice; season with salt and pepper. (The remaining smoked oil will keep for several weeks.)

Chop the reserved fennel sprigs and mix them by hand in a separate bowl with the goat cheese and red-pepper threads until fully incorporated. Roll into six uniformly sized balls.

Divide the mixed vegetables evenly among six plates. Add two beet wedges and a goat cheese marble to each and sprinkle toasted pecans evenly over the top. Serve immediately.

S'MORES-STYLE SPRING ROLLS WITH STRAWBERRY-GINGER DIPPING SAUCE

(SERVES 6)

12 spring roll wrappers

6 ounces (about 3 cups) mini marshmallows

3 ounces (about ½ cup) chocolate chips

3 ounces graham crackers, crushed (about 1 cup)

8 ounces fresh strawberries, trimmed and halved (about 2 cups)

2 cups sugar

¼ cup plus 1 teaspoon water

1 tablespoon ginger juice (available at specialty markets)

1 teaspoon cornstarch

½ gallon (8 cups) vegetable oil

Special equipment:

frying thermometer

In a pot, heat enough water to dip the wrappers; when very hot but not boiling, remove from stovetop. Combine the marshmallows, chocolate chips, and graham crackers in a bowl. Place one wrapper into the water for 30 seconds; transfer to a clean cutting board. Place ¼ cup marshmallow mixture in the center of the wrapper; fold in the sides and roll up like a burrito. Place on a sheet tray in the refrigerator and repeat with the remaining wrappers.

Place the strawberries, sugar, ¼ cup water, and ginger juice in a saucepan over high heat and cook for 8 minutes; meanwhile, mix the cornstarch and remaining teaspoon water in a small bowl until thoroughly combined. Whisk the cornstarch mixture into the pan and cook for 2 more minutes; remove from heat and let cool. Transfer to a blender and pulse until smooth.

In a heavy-bottomed pot, heat oil to 350°F. Drop in a spring roll and fry for 45 seconds or until golden brown; repeat with the remaining rolls. Serve immediately on a platter with a bowl of strawberry-ginger sauce for dipping.

Jax Fish House & Oyster Bar

928 Pearl Street
Boulder, CO 80302
(303) 444-1811
JAXBOULDER.COM

1539 17th Street
Denver, CO 80202
(303) 292-5767
JAXDENVER.COM
OWNER: DAVE QUERY
CHEF: SHEILA LUCERO

Back in 1994, when Colorado was still saddled with a ranchland repertoire that amounted to beef, beans, and beer, Jax opened its doors onto Boulder's Pearl Street Mall—and immediately proved that a slice of the coastal life was just what the landlocked locals needed. A year later, the smash hit spawned a LoDo sibling—and both branches just keep cruising smoothly along to this day (in fact, a Fort Collins outpost is now bustling as well, and a Cherry Creek spot should be open by press time).

A positively buoyant dockside vibe plays no small role in their enduring popularity, occupying as they do long, narrow spaces that the happy-hour crowd packs like (what else?) sardines. On the graffiti-scrawled brick walls hangs all manner of pisciform bric-a-brac; wooden planks turn the ceilings into upside-down jetties; aquariums shimmer. And it all points, of course, to exuberant cuisine informed but hardly limited by the daily catch. Clam chowder made brand-new with fresh pork belly and pumpkin, for instance. Or gussied-up hush puppies with shrimp in *beurre blanc*. Or the ever-changing but always winning blackened catfish, now perched atop buckwheat waffles, now accompanied by skillet bread and corn relish. Meanwhile, the keepers of the island bars dole out oysters on the half-shell like nobody's business, along with Bloody Marys that'll give you your sea legs—only to knock 'em right out from under you.

Ahi Tuna with Fingerling Potato–Andouille Hash & Grana Padano Vinaigrette

(SERVES 4)

For the vinaigrette:

½ teaspoon Dijon mustard

½ teaspoon minced garlic

2 tablespoons cider vinegar

3 tablespoons extra-virgin olive oil

⅓ cup Grana Padano cheese, grated

Salt and pepper to taste

1 red bell pepper

Olive oil as directed

4 (6-ounce) portions of #1 sashimi-grade ahi tuna

Salt and pepper as directed

1 pound fingerling potatoes, scrubbed

1 Vidalia onion, peeled and quartered

½ cup dry, light white wine, such as Sauvignon
    Blanc or Chablis

Juice of ½ lemon

½ cup water

1 sprig thyme

2 sprigs parsley

1 tablespoon sugar

½ pound andouille sausage, removed from casing
    and crumbled

4 tablespoons vegetable oil, divided

8 ounces watercress, rinsed and destemmed

Special equipment:

outdoor grill (optimal)

To make the vinaigrette, place the mustard, garlic, and vinegar in a small mixing bowl. Whisk to combine, then slowly whisk in the oil. Add cheese, season with salt and pepper to taste, and set aside.

Coat the red pepper in olive oil and roast over a hot grill, or blacken it without oil over a gas-burner flame. When the skin is fully charred, remove the

pepper from the heat source to cool, then remove the skin and seeds and julienne. Set aside.

Season tuna portions with salt and pepper and place in the refrigerator until ready to cook.

In a medium-size pot, cover fingerlings with salted water. Bring to a boil and simmer for about 20 minutes, or until potatoes are tender. Drain and let cool, then quarter potatoes lengthwise.

Preheat the oven to 350°F. In a small baking dish, combine onion, white wine, lemon juice, water, thyme, parsley, and sugar. Cover with foil and roast for 90 minutes; when done, onion layers should be tender and pull away easily. Strain liquid and set aside to cool.

In a large sauté pan over medium heat, render sausage until cooked but not crispy. Remove sausage, set aside, and pour out excess grease. Add 2 tablespoons vegetable oil and cooled potatoes; cook until golden, about 4–5 minutes.

Meanwhile, heat the remaining vegetable oil in a separate pan over medium-high heat. Add tuna and sear for 1 minute on each side. Remove and set aside.

Add sausage and onion "petals" to pan with potatoes. Continue to cook over medium heat for 2–3 minutes. Pull from heat and add julienned red pepper.

Transfer the mixture to a large bowl. Add watercress, toss, and season with salt and pepper to taste, then add the vinaigrette.

Divide hash equally among four plates. Slice each portion of tuna into four pieces and lay on top of hash.

A COLLEGE TOWN'S EPICUREAN EDUCATION

Though a staff writer on the food beat at the *Denver Post,* Douglas Brown happens to reside in Boulder—and thus has witnessed firsthand the erstwhile hippie enclave's rapid transformation into a dining destination worthy of the honorific "America's Foodiest Town" (as bestowed by *Bon Appétit* in 2010).

Between the magnificent and quirky Flatirons nearly hanging over the city, the historic downtown, the maze of bike and pedestrian paths, and the charming University of Colorado campus, Boulder may be the best-looking town along the Front Range.

Unfortunately, the sexy little city didn't always know how to eat. For a long time, our dining options were limited to burgers, pizza, take-out Chinese, *saag paneer* at an Indian or Nepalese buffet, wings. But that changed rapidly in

the 2000s, when every week, it seemed, a new and ambitious restaurant opened its doors: The Kitchen (pictured here and featured on page 94), for one, launched a movement to go local, go organic, keep it simple, do it well—and restaurants like Black Cat Bistro (page 32) and SALT (1047 Pearl Street; 303-444-7258; saltboulderbistro.com) followed. Frasca Food and Wine (page 68) explored the foods of Friuli, Italy, with a daunting intensity; Centro Latin Kitchen & Refreshment Palace (950 Pearl Street; 303-442-7771; centrolatinkitchen.com) gave us a taste of Central and South America, and L'Atelier (1739 Pearl Street; 303-442-7233; latelierboulder.com) did the same for contemporary France.

Today, the Pearl Street Mall still dominates the dining scene, but there is too much chefly talent to remain confined for long. Boulder's still-young reputation for interesting food began on the edges of the tourist strip, and that's where it is likely to continue. Cured (page 54), a charcuterie, cheese, and wine emporium on the eastern fringes of Pearl, is thriving; let's hope the food-obsessed continue to congregate on that side of the street. The charming western edge is now home to Beehive (2018 10th Street; 303-786-8585; beehivegoodness.com), a lovely vest-pocket of a place with a solid menu in the locavore vein, and Zoe Ma Ma (2010 10th Street; 303-545-MAMA; zoemama.com), an even smaller vest-pocket that serves Chinese street food, as prepared by a real-deal grandmother. Here, too, there's room for growth.

Either way, a trip to Boulder no longer needs to hinge entirely on the surrounding beauty. Come to hike, to sightsee, to take pictures—and most definitely to eat.

JENNA JOHANSEN

JENNAJOHANSEN.COM
THELASTTHINGWEATE.COM

While outsiders know her from her stint on Season 1 of Bravo's reality cooking-competition series *Around the World in 80 Plates,* Coloradans knew Jenna Johansen first—namely as the acclaimed chef-partner of Dish in Edwards.

The Greeley-born, Boulder-raised toque has since left the restaurant and the Vail area to settle in Denver as a freelance consultant and culinary instructor with husband Mark DeNittis, himself a master butcher and salumi producer; together they run the blog *The Last Thing We Ate* and cook at local charity events, which "really makes me happy," she says. In short, she's taking some time to "nurture my creativity and investigate my motivations. Now that I'm here, I'm not going anywhere; this is where my family is. So I'm avidly looking for a new home in the kitchen."

Which begs the question, why not open a place with DeNittis? On that topic, Johansen remains coy: "It's so possible; you never know. We've been bouncing ideas off each other since the day we met, so it's a natural fit." The following recipe is a perfect example. "Mark and I talk about sausage a lot," she laughs. "I'm passionate about it too, and I fell in love with this one while traveling in Thailand because it incorporates rice, which gives it such a fascinating texture." Though it's typically fermented, she has simplified the recipe for home cooks.

Sai Krok

ISAAN SOUR SAUSAGE

Ask your butcher for the appropriate length of hog casing to make two pounds of sausage (you will probably need about 4 feet). You should be able to locate *sambal oelek,* an Indonesian chili paste, at any Asian market along with sticky rice. Note that this recipe takes a few days to complete.

(MAKES ABOUT 8 LARGER LINKS OR 16 SMALLER LINKS)

For the sausage:

2 pounds ground pork
2 cups sticky (glutinous) rice, cooked according
    to package directions and cooled
¼ cup cilantro, finely chopped
1½ tablespoons minced garlic
1 tablespoon minced scallions
1 tablespoon grated fresh ginger
2 limes, zested and juiced
2 tablespoons fish sauce
2 teaspoons white pepper
½ teaspoon cayenne pepper
32- to 35-millimiter hog casing
Grapeseed oil as directed

For garnish (per large link; adjust as necessary):

About 1 tablespoon chopped peanuts
About 1 teaspoon chopped cilantro
1 Bibb or butter lettuce leaf
Sambal oelek to taste
1 lime wedge

Special equipment:

large pastry bag
meat thermometer

To make the sausage: Mix by hand all ingredients (except casing and oil) in a large bowl until well combined.

Place a small amount of the mixture in a small, hot pan and cook through. Taste and adjust the seasoning of the uncooked mixture as desired before transferring it to your pastry bag.

Rinse the hog casing in warm water. Ideally with the help of an assistant, begin to pipe the sausage into the casing, twisting at 2-inch intervals for smaller (and more traditional) sausages, or at 6-inch intervals if you prefer bun-sized links. When finished, make sure both ends are knotted tightly. Store sausages in the refrigerator for 2–3 days prior to cooking. (Their color may lighten in the meantime; if so, do not be concerned.)

Though it may also be grilled or roasted, Johansen prefers pan-seared *sai krok.* Add grapeseed oil to lightly but evenly coat a pan over high heat; when it is very hot, reduce to medium and cook the sausages, turning regularly to avoid burning, until they reach an internal temperature of 165°F (check with thermometer), about 6–8 minutes. (*Note:* Do not overcrowd the pan; rather, cook links in batches with additional oil as necessary.)

To serve: Sprinkle sausages with peanuts and cilantro, accompanied by lettuce leaves for wrapping, *sambal,* and lime wedges.

JONESY'S EATBAR

400 EAST 20TH AVENUE
DENVER, CO 80205
(303) 863-7473
JEATBAR.COM
OWNERS: LEIGH JONES AND MARGARET MOORE
CHEF: ALEXANDRIA WHITE

Nobody doesn't get a kick out of Jonesy's. At the edge of a tiny park on the outskirts of downtown, it stands where a midcentury pharmacy complete with soda fountain once must have lured teenyboppers by the gaggle; now hipsters pack the three-room haunt to soak up its vintage style. "We had to piece it together on a shoestring," says co-owner Leigh Jones, "but we've finally got the Jonesy's we want." Several crimson plush booths were salvaged from the closure of long-standing red-sauce joint Pagliacci's; period kitsch dots the gorgeous Art Deco–era bar (think parlor lamps with owl-shaped bases); old family photos line walls whose yellowish cast amusingly suggests nicotine stains "from customers who'd have been smoking here back in the day"; a small bookshelf and a stack of board games bid regulars feel at home.

So, of course, does the gastropub-inspired menu. Loaded fries and sliders in cheeky array are its signatures, but seasonal comforts from chef Alex White (pictured left) rarely fail to hit the spot: Garlicky mixed-mushroom tapenade on toast or crisp-skinned duck-leg confit over rice pudding generate deep-down warmth, as do sausage grits and chicken-fried pork come Sunday brunch. The bar, meanwhile, takes local sourcing to its ripping extreme. Some forty beers bearing the labels of Front Range favorites like Avery and Dry Dock appear on tap, in bottle, and in cocktails that also contain native sodas, liqueurs, and spirits (which may be infused with green chiles, tamarind syrup, or roasted peanuts and honey); even the short wine list is largely dedicated to Western Slope producers like Settembre Cellars and Jack Rabbit Hill.

For all its nostalgic underpinnings, then, Jonesy's is ultimately a toast to the Colorado high life in the here and now. We come to lift our glass.

St. Louis–Style Gooey Butter Cake

(SERVES 7–8)

1 box yellow cake mix, preferably Duncan Hines
1½ cups butter, melted, plus extra for greasing the pan
Juice and zest of 2 lemons
½ cup water
3 eggs
4 ounces cream cheese, softened
1 tablespoon vanilla extract
2 cups confectioners' sugar
Unsweetened whipped cream and sliced strawberries
    for garnish

Special equipment:
hand mixer
9-inch square baking pan

Preheat the oven to 300°F.

Place cake mix, melted butter, lemon juice, and water in a large mixing bowl and blend with a hand mixer on low speed for 3 minutes.

In a separate bowl, combine lemon zest, eggs, cream cheese, and vanilla with the mixer on low speed until smooth. Slowly add sugar until the consistency is velvety, about 3–4 minutes.

Grease a 9-inch square baking pan with butter. Spoon the cake mixture evenly into the pan so the surface is level, then carefully layer the cream-cheese mixture on top. Bake for 30 minutes; remove from oven and let cool 20 minutes. Cut into pieces and garnish as desired with whipped cream and strawberries.

Autumn Sangria

This recipe uses the products of two Colorado distilleries, Leopold Bros. and Dancing Pines; both are readily available at area liquor stores. It also relies on an exclusive house wine from Boulder's BookCliff Vineyards, charmingly labeled Jonesy's Blushing Beauty—but most any rosé will do.

(SERVES 1)

3 ounces off-dry rosé of your choice
1½ ounces Leopold Bros. New York Apple Whiskey
½ ounce Dancing Pines Chai Liqueur
Generous splash of ginger ale

Carefully pour rosé, whiskey, and liqueur into a large wine glass filled partway with ice and stir to combine. Top with ginger ale.

THE KITCHEN

1039 PEARL STREET
BOULDER, CO 80302
(720) 542-8159

1530 16TH STREET
DENVER, CO 80202
(303) 623-3127
THEKITCHENCOMMUNITY.COM
CHEFS/OWNERS: HUGO MATHESON AND KIMBAL MUSK
CO-OWNER: JEN LEWIN; CHEF: KYLE MENDENHALL
CHEF DE CUISINE, BOULDER: DENNIS PHELPS
CHEF DE CUISINE, DENVER: GABE GODELL

The deceptively generic name says it all. Certainly it speaks to the interior design, a simple affair of rough-hewn wood and stone, blackboards mounted on red brick, and bright yellow-and-blue floor tiles that, centered on a chandelier-lit communal table, exudes the convivial ease of family meals gone by. More importantly, though, it points to the back of a house whose emphasis is not on the cult of chefly personality but rather on the spirit of cooperation among cooks, bakers, growers, ranchers, and so on: kitchen as way station between farm and dining room.

Opening on Boulder's Pearl Street Mall in 2004, the restaurant quickly gained national attention as an eco-pioneer: Founders Hugo Matheson, Kimbal Musk, and Jen Lewin not only salvaged much of the building material but implemented wind power as well as recycling and composting programs that, to this day, ensure waste is virtually nil, be it corks or cooking oil. In 2011, they formed a nonprofit organization to nurture "learning gardens" across the nation; today, these outdoor classrooms are being tended by

schoolchildren from Los Angeles to Chicago. Still, gastronomes cannot live on green initiatives alone. All that organic produce, sustainably raised meat, biodynamic wine, and microbrew have to come together in ways that taste good. And they do. Stylish in its very rusticity, the seasonal menu juxtaposes craft and comfort to captivating effect. Chargrilled squid is tossed with arugula and bathed in the warm herbed olive-oil sauce known to Italians as *salmoriglio*. Cumin-scented yogurt enriches a mélange of winter squash and wheat berries. Brightly bitter notes of kale, hazelnut, and *gremolata* hone *agnolotti* stuffed with braised beef. And the sticky toffee pudding—a nod to Matheson's rural English upbringing—is a hearty marvel.

Today, The Kitchen stands the flagship of a multi-unit enterprise. There's a cozy second-floor lounge, The Kitchen [Upstairs]; an adjacent gastropub, The Kitchen [Next Door], and a gorgeous outpost in Denver's LoDo district—all imbued by a distinctive sense of place, where farmhouse meets townhouse meets second home.

CASSOULET

This dish takes two or three days to make from start to finish, but the sausage can be made at any time, as it freezes well (you will have a few extra).

(SERVES 6)

For the sausage:

10 black peppercorns

5 allspice berries

4 juniper berries

1 piece star anise

2 pounds pork shoulder

½ pound pork fatback

7 cloves garlic, minced

2 tablespoons fresh chopped sage

1 tablespoon fresh chopped thyme

½ cup plus 1 splash brandy, divided

1⅓ tablespoons salt

10 natural hog casings (available at your local butcher shop)

For the duck confit:

6 pieces star anise

¼ cup juniper berries

2 tablespoons ground allspice

2 tablespoons black pepper

1 tablespoon red pepper flakes

1 cup kosher salt

1 cup sugar

6 duck legs

1 quart duck fat (available at specialty markets)

For the cassoulet base:

1 tablespoon duck fat

6 ounces slab smoked bacon

3 cloves garlic, slivered

1 cup medium-dice onion

1 cup medium-dice celery root

1 cup medium-dice carrot

Salt as directed

1½ cups dry red wine

1 bay leaf

1 sprig thyme

5 black peppercorns

1 clove

1 (16-ounce) can peeled tomatoes, roughly crushed

3 cups beef or chicken stock

3 cups cooked white beans (may be canned)

Pepper to taste

For the bread crumbs:

¼ cup duck fat

Small loaf french bread

2 tablespoons chopped thyme

Special equipment:

spice grinder or mortar and pestle

cheesecloth or tea ball

kitchen twine (optional)

large-hole funnel

On day one, start the sausage: Grind the whole spices in a spice grinder or mortar with a pestle. Cube the pork products and place in a good-size bowl; add the ground spices, garlic, herbs, ½ cup brandy, and salt and marinate in the refrigerator, covered, overnight.

Next, make the duck confit: In a dry pan over medium-low heat, lightly toast the star anise, juniper berries, allspice, black pepper, and red pepper flakes just until aromatic. Grind in a spice grinder (or use a mortar and pestle), then mix in a shallow bowl with the salt and sugar to combine. Carefully press the duck legs into the seasoning mixture until fully and evenly coated. Place them in a shallow container, wrap, and let cure in the fridge overnight.

For the cassoulet base: Brown 1 tablespoon duck fat in a heavy-bottom pot over a medium burner; when hot (but not smoking), add the bacon slab and brown on both sides. Throw in the garlic

and cook a minute until fragrant; then add the diced root vegetables with a pinch of salt and sauté 5–8 minutes, until just tender. Add the wine and reduce by three-fourths (about 5 minutes, though eyeballing the volume will be your most accurate measure). Meanwhile, place the bay leaf, thyme sprig, peppercorns, and clove in a cheesecloth sachet fastened with twine or in a tea ball.

When the liquid in the pot has reduced, add tomatoes, stock, white beans, and the herb sachet or ball to the pot. Simmer 2 hours over low heat, stirring occasionally and seasoning with salt and pepper to taste (bear in mind you will be adding well-seasoned meats later on). At this point, remove the bacon and chop it into pieces, then return it to the pot and place the whole thing in the refrigerator overnight to develop flavors.

On day two: Preheat the oven to 250°F. Transfer the duck legs to a clean, shallow, ovenproof dish in which they fit snugly. Cover them with the quart of duck fat, wrap dish with aluminum foil, and cook for 5 hours. Remove and cool in the refrigerator, still submerged in the fat.

Meanwhile, finish the sausage: Fill a bowl large enough to hold the bowl containing the sausage mixture with ice. Transfer the mixture to a food processor; grind finely, then return it to its bowl, add a splash of brandy, place the bowl over the ice to keep the meat cool, and mix with your hands to achieve a tacky texture. Chill for several hours, then use a large-hole funnel to push the sausage into the hog casings with your hands, making 10 links of about 4 ounces each. Knot both ends of the casing (or tie with twine if you prefer) and store 6 links in the refrigerator until ready to use; freeze the remaining 4 for future use.

To make the bread crumbs: Melt ¼ cup duck fat over medium heat in a small pot. Cut the french loaf into pieces, place in a food processor, and

pulse into coarse crumbs; add the duck fat and chopped thyme and pulse to combine.

Preheat the oven to 300°F. Place the cassoulet base in a large, ovenproof casserole dish; stir in 6 sausages (they can be chopped or left whole) and duck legs, then cover the surface with bread crumbs. Bake 30–40 minutes until the sausages are cooked through and a golden crust forms; the consistency should be stew-like. Serve in bowls, each containing a duck leg and an equal amount of sausage.

GRILLED BROCCOLI WITH ANCHOÏADE DRESSING

Says executive chef de cuisine Dennis Phelps (pictured on page 94), "This is a different way to eat broccoli, either on its own or with some grilled fish. We like to use the stalks, as they are just as good as the florets. The dressing can also be made as we do in the restaurant, in a mortar and pestle."

If you don't have an outdoor grill, preheat your oven to 500°F, season the broccoli as directed without blanching it, and roast for approximately 10 minutes.

(SERVES 6)

For the dressing:

2 tablespoons finely chopped fresh rosemary
1 large clove garlic, finely chopped
1 (2-ounce) tin anchovy fillets, drained
⅓ cup extra-virgin olive oil
Juice of 2 lemons

For the broccoli:

2–3 pounds broccoli, stalks on (preferably organic)
Olive oil to drizzle
Salt and black pepper
Lemon wedges for garnish

Special equipment:

outdoor grill (optional)

To make the dressing: Place the rosemary and garlic in a food processor and add the anchovies. While the motor is running, slowly add olive oil until you obtain a smooth paste. Add lemon juice and set aside for a couple of hours at room temperature to meld the flavors.

To make the broccoli: If the skin on the broccoli stalks is very thick, peel off the outer layer. Trim the bottom of the stalk and cut the broccoli lengthwise into wedges, or separate into large florets.

Bring 6 quarts of well-salted water to a boil. Drop in the broccoli and allow the water to come back to a gentle boil. Cook until al dente, about 5 minutes. Strain and set aside. If you are not serving right away, place it in a bowl in the refrigerator to cool.

Before grilling, dry the broccoli as best as you can, then toss with a little olive oil and season with salt and pepper to taste.

Heat the grill and cook the broccoli about 4–5 minutes, turning carefully once or twice until it gets a nice char and the florets develop an appealing crispy texture.

Place the broccoli on a serving dish with some lemon wedges and drizzle with the *anchoïade*.

Lala's Wine Bar + Pizzeria

410 East 7th Avenue
Denver, CO 80203
(303) 861-9463
LALASWINEBAR.COM
Owners: Mike Plancarte and John Ott; Chef: Samir Mohammad

That Lala's is named for a turn-of-the-century socialite who, with her father Walter Scott Cheesman, built the Governor's Mansion just a block or so up Capitol Hill is only fitting. After all, come happy hour on any given evening, this neighborhood place par excellence swarms with the butterflies of today. Even in winter, heat lamps draw them in clusters to the patio adjoining the long dining room, which shimmers in the warmth of terra-cotta-toned, cork-accented walls and amber-glass light fixtures, bordered by a bar that, though packed, always seems to accommodate just one more body.

There the fast-moving crew dispenses dozens of wines on tap—among them such appealingly smart finds as the Italian white Grechetto, sparkling Pinot Noir from Spain, and Coloradan Petit Verdot—while whipping up fun seasonal cocktails spiked with house-infused syrups. At the far end of the room, the white-tiled open kitchen bustles with activity, overseen by rising star Samir Mohammad (pictured), to yield solidly crafted pizzas like the *vongole,* made with clams, ricotta *salata,* fennel, and artichoke hearts—but also some rather underrated antipasti and *tramezzini* (cousins to panini).

We adore, for instance, the flatbread wedges accompanied by eye-rollingly rich spreads like textbook chicken-liver mousse and mascarpone swirled with pungent arugula pesto, as well as truffled polenta fries accompanied by smoked Gorgonzola cream. But Mohammad also makes one angry meatball on ciabatta slathered with spicy aioli, and his *dolci* defy resistance, from blueberry-filled *bomboloni* (doughnuts) to peach–butter pecan gelato.

Anger and defiance are not, however, Lala's modi operandi. As co-owner Mike Plancarte puts it, "We really want to take care of the neighborhood's needs. People come for special occasions; they bring their young families; they pop in just to have a glass of wine by themselves." Granted, those loners may well wind up chatting away with a fellow oenophile or sports fan catching the game on the TVs mounted above the bar. That's just the kind of gathering spot this is.

CAULIFLOWER GNOCCHI WITH ROASTED KALE & LIMONCELLO BROTH

Start this recipe a few hours in advance to give the gnocchi time to chill (they will keep frozen for up to six months).

(SERVES 6–8)

1 head cauliflower, trimmed

2 tablespoons plus 1 teaspoon butter

½ cup water

1 teaspoon kosher salt, plus extra as directed

⅛ teaspoon black pepper, plus extra as directed

1 cup ricotta

1 whole egg plus 1 egg yolk

2–2½ cups high-gluten flour, plus extra for dusting

1 tablespoon diced chives

1 tablespoon olive oil

For the limoncello broth:

½ cup limoncello

1 cup chicken stock

1 tablespoon butter

Salt and pepper to taste

For the roasted kale:

½ pound kale, trimmed, rinsed well, and dried

3 tablespoons olive oil

1 teaspoon kosher salt

Chop cauliflower into bite-size (about 1-inch) florets and place in a lidded pot over medium heat with 2 tablespoons butter, water, 1 teaspoon salt, and ⅛ teaspoon pepper. Cover and steam until tender, about 15 minutes. Place 1 cup in blender or food processor and puree. Reserve the remaining cauliflower.

Place pureed cauliflower, ricotta, egg and yolk, 2 cups flour, and chives into a large mixing bowl, season with salt and pepper, and gently fold the ingredients until you achieve a firm but slightly sticky dough (add more flour as necessary).

Lightly flour a clean counter surface and, by hand, roll the dough into ½-inch-thick logs. Cut the logs into pieces about 1 inch long and roll to coat in the flour. Place on a flour-dusted sheet pan, making sure they are not touching, and place them uncovered in the freezer to chill.

Meanwhile, to make the broth, place limoncello in medium saucepan and bring to a simmer; reduce by half. Add stock and simmer for 3 more minutes, then turn heat off. Add butter, salt, and pepper and set aside.

To prepare the kale, preheat the oven to 400°F. Place kale leaves, olive oil, and salt in a large bowl and massage for 2 minutes, until well mixed. Place on sheet pan and bake 8–10 minutes or until crispy.

Place a sauté pan over medium heat. When hot, add remaining teaspoon butter and 1 tablespoon olive oil. Place chilled gnocchi in sauté pan and let cook for about 4 minutes or until brown; then flip over and cook another 3 minutes. Add the limoncello broth and simmer for about 3 minutes. Add the reserved cauliflower and season to taste. Serve in bowls topped with roasted kale.

Date-Walnut Cake with Toffee Sauce

Start this recipe several hours in advance.

(SERVES 8–10)

1¼ cups dates, pitted and chopped
(Mohammad prefers large, soft Medjools)

1½ cups water

2 teaspoons baking soda

⅔ cup sugar

½ pound unsalted butter, room temperature,
plus extra for greasing

2 teaspoons vanilla extract

4 large eggs

2½ cups flour

2 teaspoons baking powder

Pinch of salt

1½ cups chopped walnuts

For the toffee sauce:

1 cup water

½ cup brandy

2 cups brown sugar

1 tablespoon honey

Special equipment:

hand mixer

10-inch springform pan

Preheat the oven to 375°F.

Place chopped dates in a medium saucepan with water; bring to a simmer and add the baking soda. Turn off the heat and let sit for 5 minutes.

With a hand mixer on medium speed, cream together sugar and butter in a large bowl for 5 minutes. Add vanilla and eggs; mix on medium-high speed for an additional 3 minutes.

In a medium bowl, combine flour, baking powder, and salt. Add the dry ingredients gradually to the egg mixture, mixing continuously on low speed; do the same with the dates. Once the ingredients are fully combined, mix on medium for 2 minutes. Gently fold in the walnuts.

Place cake batter into springform pan greased with butter and bake for 35–45 minutes (insert a toothpick to check for doneness; it should emerge clean). Remove from oven and allow cake to cool for 20 minutes.

Meanwhile, prepare the toffee sauce: Bring water and brandy to a simmer in a large pot. Add brown sugar and honey; simmer for 3 minutes to obtain a thin syrup.

Using a chopstick or skewer, poke multiple holes into the surface of the cake and pour toffee sauce on top. Let the cake sit in the pan at room temperature, covered, at least 5 hours before cutting.

LAO WANG NOODLE HOUSE

945 SOUTH FEDERAL BOULEVARD
DENVER, CO 80219
(303) 975-2497
CHEFS/OWNERS: TSE-MING WANG AND CHUN-MING WANG

Behind the most nondescript of storefronts on Federal lies a treasure trove of luscious soup dumplings, potstickers, and wontons, noodle bowls and marinated pork shanks and chili-shocked veggies. It's a family joint, a darling of critics, and a chefs' hangout alike; you could ask just about anyone in town about it and receive an impassioned impromptu ode to its tiny kitchen in return. Better yet, you can get the inside scoop from the owners' son, Danny Wang of CAUTION: Brewing Co. (12445 East 39th Avenue, Unit 314, Denver; 970-315-BREW; cautionbrewingco.com)—whose flagship Lao Wang Lager just so

happens to boast their secret house blend of spices.

"My parents are from Xindian, Taiwan," he'll tell you. "We arrived in 1985, and my dad worked up and down the Front Range as a chef before opening his own place in 1999. My dad is an absolute perfectionist; he never cuts corners and always uses the best ingredients he can get. Coming here is like going home. It's intimate, cozy, and very traditional, with the menu in Mandarin on the walls; it's always packed, and the food will never be rushed—but as at home, you should respect your parents! They'll never apologize for not representing the norm; remember it's only the two of them working sixty-plus hours a week—and the cooking will speak volumes about who they are."

If that's the case, they must be remarkable people.

Chinese Cold Noodles with Chicken

The meat is optional; vegetarians may simply omit it. You should be able to find white sesame sauce at local Asian markets like Pacific Ocean Marketplace (2200 West Alameda Avenue, Denver; 303-936-4845; pacificoceanmarket.com); if not, peanut butter is a fine substitute.

(SERVES 4)

For the noodle sauce:

1 cube chicken bouillon dissolved in 1 cup
    boiling water, cooled
¼ cup soy sauce
1 tablespoon sugar
3–5 drops white vinegar

For the sesame or peanut sauce:

6 ounces white sesame sauce or 4 ounces creamy
    peanut butter
Water as directed

2 skinless, bone-in chicken breasts
1 pound dried Chinese noodles or long pasta
2 ounces (about 1 large) carrot, shaved with a peeler
2 ounces (about 6 large) white radish, shaved with
    a peeler
Minced garlic to taste
Chili oil to taste

To make the noodle sauce, combine all ingredients well in a bowl; store in refrigerator until needed.

If you are making peanut sauce, simply whisk the peanut butter together with a small amount of water, adding a few drops at a time as necessary until the mixture is the consistency of salad dressing, neither too thin nor too thick. Store in refrigerator. (The sesame sauce is ready-made and does not need to be adjusted.)

Bring a pot of water to a boil, add the chicken breasts, and boil for 30 minutes or until cooked through. Let cool, then shred the meat and store in the refrigerator.

Bring another pot of salted water to a boil, cook noodles according to package instructions until al dente, and drain. (If you will not be serving them immediately, toss them with a teaspoon of neutral cooking oil and place in the refrigerator.)

To serve, divide noodles among four plates. Top with even amounts of shredded chicken, carrot and radish shavings, cold noodle sauce, and sesame or peanut sauce. Instruct your fellow diners to mix it all together and add minced garlic and chili oil to taste!

LEAF VEGETARIAN RESTAURANT

2010 16TH STREET
BOULDER, CO 80302
(303) 442-1485
LEAFVEGETARIANRESTAURANT.COM
OWNERS: LENNY MARTINELLI, SARA MARTINELLI, AND
JERRY MANNING; CHEF: RACHEL BEST

Merely to cross the threshold of this low-profile eatery off Boulder's main dining drag is to instantly feel uplifted, centered, healthier. Sunlight pours through the windows of the dining room, clean and serene in shades of pale green and eggshell; blond woods gleam; cutworked ball-pendant lights cast intricate shadows; an undulating copper fountain burbles. And a glance at the menu only heightens the sensation of vitality.

Making its own tofu and seitan while obtaining produce from the proprietors' ten-acre Three Leaf Farm in nearby Lafayette, the kitchen develops an array of seasonal dishes whose wholesomeness is a given— but whose contemporary verve comes as a delightful surprise. Gone are the dour clichés of American vegetarianism circa 1975, à la Woody Allen's "mashed yeast and sprouts" in *Annie Hall;* in their place, diverse plates from chef Rachel Best (pictured) burst into bloom. Co-owner Sara Martinelli calls the sesame-encrusted "beet steak," touched with wasabi cream on a bed of garlic mashed potatoes, one of her "favorite dishes of all time"; we might say the same of the fat, luscious mushroom-walnut burger topped with provolone and kicky remoulade on whole wheat toast. Some preparations contain eggs as well as cheese, others are wholly vegan and/or raw—but all abound in festive touches, be it roasted winter squash stuffed with ricotta, quinoa, almonds, cranberries, spinach, and polenta croutons; robust heirloom bean-and-hominy cakes over swirls of pumpkin puree and brown butter; or succulent carrot cake with soy-cream frosting and candied ginger. Leaf teas and refreshing virgin sippers like the hibiscus cooler round out a full bar that emphasizes local spirits and sustainably produced wines.

We can't swear you'll leave here smarter, stronger, and sexier than you were when you came in, but it will sure feel that way.

Apricot Deviled Eggs

(SERVES 4–6)

12 eggs
1 tablespoon plus 1½ teaspoons salt, plus extra to taste
¼ cup nondairy mayonnaise
¼ cup apricot preserves
½ teaspoon pepper, plus extra to taste
¼ teaspoon paprika
8 ounces arugula, washed, dried, and trimmed
Olive oil as directed
1 fresh apricot, slivered (optional)

Special equipment:

pastry bag (optional)

Place eggs with 1 tablespoon salt in a good-size pot and cover with cold water. Bring to a boil and cook for 8 minutes, then immediately remove from the heat and put ice in the pot; as soon as eggs have cooled, peel them.

Slice eggs in half lengthwise, carefully removing the yolks. Place yolks, 1½ teaspoons salt, mayonnaise, preserves, ½ teaspoon pepper, and paprika in a food processor and blend until smooth. Put the filling in a pastry bag (or you can use a ziplock bag with a small hole cut from one bottom corner) and pipe the yolk mixture into the hollows of the egg whites.

In a bowl, toss arugula in a small amount of olive oil and season with salt and pepper to taste. Transfer to a serving platter and place eggs on top of greens. Garnish each with a sliver of apricot if desired.

Jamaican Jerk Tempeh with Black Rice, Coconut-Plantain Sauce & Fruit Salsa

(SERVES 8)

For the fruit salsa:

1 cup fresh fruit of your choice, such as mango, pear, strawberries, or blackberries, peeled if necessary and diced small

1 small red onion, diced

1 jalapeño, minced

1 tablespoon minced garlic

⅛ cup fresh lime juice

3 tablespoons minced fresh cilantro

2 teaspoons ground cumin

1 tablespoon minced fresh ginger

Salt and pepper to taste

For the tempeh:

1 red onion, chopped

3 scallions, chopped

5 jalapeño peppers, seeded and chopped

2 tablespoons chopped garlic

1 tablespoon white sugar

1 tablespoon ground allspice

1 tablespoon dried thyme

1½ teaspoons salt

1½ teaspoons cayenne pepper

1½ teaspoons black pepper

¾ teaspoon nutmeg

½ teaspoon cinnamon

¾ cup cider vinegar

½ cup orange juice

¼ cup lime juice

¼ cup canola oil

¼ cup tamari

4 (8- to 10-ounce) packages block tempeh

For the coconut-plantain sauce:

2 tablespoons vegetable oil

¼ yellow onion, chopped

1 green plantain, peeled and cut into ¼-inch slices (available at Latin markets)

2 tablespoons dry white wine

1 teaspoon ground cardamom

2 large cloves fresh garlic, peeled and minced

1 stalk lemongrass

24 ounces coconut milk

½ cup orange juice

¼ cup lime juice

2 tablespoons agave nectar

1 teaspoon salt, plus extra to taste

4 cups cooked black rice (available at gourmet retailers; see package instructions for yield and method)

For the sautéed greens:

2 teaspoons canola oil

4 cups kale, chard, or collard greens, cleaned, destemmed, and torn into large pieces

¼ teaspoon minced fresh garlic

¼ cup white wine

Salt and pepper to taste

For the fruit salsa: Combine all ingredients in a mixing bowl and set aside. (Can be made in advance and stored in the refrigerator for a few days.)

To make the tempeh: Place all ingredients except tempeh in a blender and blend until smooth. Cut the tempeh blocks in half diagonally, place in a bowl, and pour in the marinade to cover. Set aside for 30–60 minutes.

Preheat the oven to 350°F.

Prepare the coconut-plantain sauce: Add vegetable oil to a good-size pot over medium heat. When hot, sauté the onion a few minutes until transparent. Add the plantain and sauté 5 minutes. Deglaze with wine until the liquid has evaporated; add the remaining ingredients and bring to a boil. Lower heat to a simmer and cook for 20 minutes. Remove the lemongrass stalk, place sauce in a blender, and blend until smooth. Adjust salt to taste.

Transfer the marinated tempeh to a cake pan and bake in the oven for 20 minutes. Meanwhile, reheat rice in the microwave, covered with a damp paper towel, or over low heat on the stove, adding a tiny bit of water as necessary for either method.

Finally, prepare the greens: Heat oil in a sauté pan over medium heat; add the greens and cook down for a minute or so, then add the remaining ingredients. Remove from heat when greens are lightly wilted and liquid has evaporated.

To serve, place a wedge of tempeh in each of eight large shallow bowls or on eight plates; add ⅓ cup warm coconut-plantain sauce and ½ cup black rice per person. Garnish as desired with sautéed greens and fruit salsa.

Le Grand Bistro & Oyster Bar

1512 Curtis Street
Denver, CO 80202
(303) 534-1155
legranddenver.com
Owner: Robert Thompson; Chef: Sergio Romero

Stateside debates about the differences between bistros and brasseries continue ad infinitum, but the takeaway is really rather simple: Brasseries are, well, brassier than bistros. With roots in German *bierhalles,* they're bigger, busier, and boozier than their quiet, cozy corner counterparts.

In that light, Le Grand—despite the official name—resembles more closely a brasserie. The sprawling downtowner sports all the telltale signs: long, mirrored bar and rows of maroon banquettes. Vintage pendant lamps and gleaming subway tiles. Dark woods, blackboards, and jaunty sketches of hog breeds labeled with their French names: *cul noir limousin, piétrain.* The repertoire, too, is broader and a touch more

freewheeling than that of your standard bistro—stretching from raw-bar, charcuterie, and cheese platters to classic steak frites and *coq au vin* to rich updates like crisped pork belly and white beans in a honey-thyme reduction, foie gras *crème brûlée* over olive-oil cake, and carrot-raisin pancakes for brunch. Meanwhile, the largely French wine list is, true to form, supplemented by local and imported beers as well as cocktails both retro and new wave, touched with such stuff as date vinegar and rose syrup.

Not to harp on semantics. In the end, Le Grand is simply itself—that warm and lively haunt we all seek out to sustain us in spirit as well as in body. *Vive la différence.*

BOUILLABAISSE

Your local fishmonger should have lobster bodies for stock, though you'd do well to call ahead. Chef Sergio Romero (pictured) recommends playing with seafood combinations, as many types of shellfish and whitefish may be included.

(SERVES 4)

¼ cup olive oil
2 yellow onions, chopped
1 carrot, peeled and chopped
2 stalks celery, chopped
1 fennel bulb, sliced
5 garlic cloves, crushed
Salt to taste
2 pounds lobster bodies, chopped
5 tomatoes, chopped
2 teaspoons saffron
2 cups dry white wine
2½ quarts vegetable stock
1 bay leaf
1 sprig thyme

1 pound whitefish fillet, cut into pieces
8 prawns or large shrimp, shelled and deveined
1 pound mussels in the shell, scrubbed and debearded
Lemon juice to taste
French bread, sliced

In a large pot, heat olive oil on medium-low heat. Add onions, carrot, celery, fennel, and garlic and cook a few minutes, until onions are tender. Season with salt, add lobster bodies, and cook until bodies have turned bright red. Next, add the tomatoes, saffron, and white wine. Turn heat to medium and cook until all the liquid has evaporated, about 15 minutes. Add vegetable stock and bring to a boil; then turn down to a simmer and cook for 1 hour, adding the bay leaf and thyme after 50 minutes.

Strain the stock mixture through a fine-mesh sieve and return to the pot (discard the solids). Bring back to a simmer and add the whitefish, then the shrimp, and finally the mussels. Once the fish is cooked and the mussels are open (about 8 minutes), remove the pot from the stove, add lemon juice as desired, divide equally among four bowls, and serve with french bread for dipping.

LOLA

1575 BOULDER STREET
DENVER, CO 80211
(720) 570-8686
LOLADENVER.COM
CHEF/CO-OWNER: JAMEY FADER
CO-OWNER: DAVE QUERY

Lola's mojo endures. Now entering its second decade, this LoHi pioneer of modern Mexican cuisine owes its staying power to an indefatigable crew who, in the words of chef-partner Jamey Fader, "takes what we do very seriously, but not ourselves. We see our job as throwing a nightly party for our guests."

That much is clear from the moment you set foot in the joint, sizzling with energy from the always-packed bar looking out onto the patio and over the downtown skyline to a dining room that trades in cantina-style tropes: rough-hewn woods, hammered copper, bubble glass, Day-Glo folk art. And it becomes even clearer with a gander at the sun-soaked, surf-sprayed seasonal menu. Seafood shines, cold or hot—start with a ceviche like the tangy, exhilarating tuna poke with pineapple, papaya, and cilantro; move on to a main as substantial and soulful as grilled shrimp and fried oysters over

sweet potato–chorizo hash smothered in pork green chile and topped with a fried egg (¡arriba! indeed). Or come for the fiesta of fun foods that is brunch: deviled eggs gone wild amid chunks of lobster and fried pancetta, adorable house-made pigs in a blanket accompanied by spicy cherry syrup, peach pancakes with a swirl of cinnamon cream and pecans. Then come back for the daily happy hour, made *muy feliz* by a serious selection of tequilas and mezcals.

"In order to keep things fresh," explains Fader, "I try to travel and pull stages in great restaurants; exposure to other chefs and new foods is the only way to go." As his armchair (or rather, barstool) companions, we couldn't agree more.

Whole Colorado Striped Bass Veracruz with Chimichurri Verde Rice & Candied Red Onions

Fader recommends tossing the extra candied onions, which will keep "forever," atop bagels with cream cheese or into salads; the leftover Veracruz sauce is great over pasta.

(SERVES 4–6)

For the candied onions:

1 cup red wine vinegar
1 cup sugar
1 red onion, julienned thin

For the Veracruz sauce:

⅓ cup olive oil
2 red onions, chopped
4 cloves garlic, roughly chopped
8 medium Roma tomatoes, sliced
3 jalapeños, sliced
⅓ cup white wine
⅓ cup sherry vinegar or red wine vinegar
4 cups canned chopped tomatoes
15–20 manzanilla olives, pitted and medium sliced
10 kalamata olives, pitted, left whole
6 caperberries, sliced lengthwise, or 2 tablespoons capers, drained
1 tablespoon chopped fresh oregano
½ bunch cilantro, cleaned and chopped
½ cup fish or chicken stock
Salt and pepper to taste
2 tablespoons fresh lime juice

For the fish:

1½ pounds whole Colorado striped bass, gutted and scaled
Extra-virgin olive oil as directed
Salt and pepper to taste
Juice of ½ lime

For the chimichurri verde rice:

2 cloves garlic, chopped
2 tablespoons red onion, chopped
2 bunches cilantro, cleaned and roughly chopped
1 bunch flat-leaf parsley, cleaned and roughly chopped
1–2 tablespoons red pepper flakes
⅓ cup red wine vinegar
2 tablespoons lemon juice
½ cup extra-virgin olive oil, plus extra as directed
Salt and pepper to taste
3 cups cooked white rice (see package for yield and cooking instructions)
Butter to taste
Juice of 1 lime

For garnish:

8–12 flour tortillas
Cilantro sprigs as desired
Lime wedges as desired

Special equipment:

outdoor grill

To make the candied onions: Place vinegar and sugar in a nonreactive pot over high heat and bring to a boil. Place onions in a nonreactive bowl, pour in the marinade, and let sit for 5–10 minutes. Strain the liquid from the bowl and place onions in refrigerator to cool.

To prepare the Veracruz sauce: Heat olive oil in a large, nonreactive pot over a medium burner, then cook onions and garlic until brown. Add sliced tomatoes and jalapeños and cook for 3 minutes; deglaze with wine and vinegar. Add canned tomatoes, olives, caperberries, herbs, and stock; lower heat to a simmer and cook for 20–25 minutes. Season with salt and pepper, then finish with lime juice. Keep warm.

For the fish: Lightly oil and start your grill, and preheat your oven to 400°F.

Score the skin of the fish by making three 1-inch cuts on both sides with a chef's knife. Drizzle the fish with olive oil and sprinkle with salt and pepper. Place fish on the grill and cook 3–5 minutes; flip and repeat. Transfer to a baking dish and finish in the oven for 15–20 minutes. Check doneness by carefully lifting the edge of one of the slits in the skin with a small knife; the flesh should no longer appear translucent. When the fish is cooked, add the lime juice.

To prepare the chimichurri rice: While the fish is in the oven, place garlic, red onion, cilantro, parsley, pepper flakes, vinegar, and lemon juice in a blender and blend. With the motor running, slowly add ½ cup olive oil and continue to blend until you've achieved the desired consistency (it can be chunky or smooth). Season to taste. Coat the bottom of a medium-size pot with olive oil and reheat the rice over a medium-low burner with butter to taste (this should take about 3–5 minutes); then stir in 1 cup chimichurri (there may be a little left over). Season with salt, pepper, and lime juice.

To serve: Warm the tortillas on a griddle (without oil). Place the rice in the center of a serving platter and lay fish on top. Ladle Veracruz sauce over the fish to smother, then sprinkle 2–3 tablespoons candied red onion on top. Garnish with cilantro sprigs and lime wedges and serve with warm, folded flour tortillas.

Los Carboncitos

720-722 Sheridan Boulevard
Denver, CO 80214
(303) 573-1617

3757 Pecos Street
Denver, CO 80211
(303) 458-0880

15210 East 6th Avenue
Aurora, CO 80011
(303) 364-2606
LOSCARBONCITOS.COM
Chefs/Owners: Ignacio León,
Cesar León, and Roberto León

Though they also run a modern, upscale eatery called Paxia (4001 Tejon Street, Denver, 720-583-6860, paxiadenver.com), where the complex pan-regional specialties of their homeland hold sway, it was at this far humbler trinity of eateries that the León brothers first found the way to locals' *corazónes* (namely, through their *estómagos*).

Here, the tireless trio puts myriad eggs in the basket of Mexico City–style cookery: The gigantic menu boasts all manner of dishes rarely seen in these parts (influenced as they mostly are by Southwestern US and northern Mexican traditions). Look for *alambres,* essentially skillet-fried mélanges of meat, vegetables, and cheese; *huaraches,* oblong masa flatbreads topped not unlike pizzas; *tortas,* which easily hold a candle to the world's greatest sandwiches; and the restaurants' tostada-esque namesake, *carboncitos*. Or don't look for them—if you're set on quesadillas, tacos, or burritos, they're available, too, in equally vast array.

Granted, once you start filling up on the quartet of notoriously fiery salsas that comes to every table with a basket of hot chips, you may not want to look at the menu at all. Lucky for you, then, that we've got the instructions for making those addictive dips right here; with a fridgeful safely squared away at home, you just might manage to give something new a try next time.

Salsa Verde

(MAKES 1 PINT)

1 pound tomatillos, skins removed, chopped
1 medium white onion, chopped
2 ounces (about 20 cloves) garlic, chopped
6 ounces (about 5–6) jalapeño peppers, destemmed, deseeded, and chopped
Salt and pepper to taste

In a pot with water to cover, boil tomatillos for 30 minutes. Transfer to a food processor; add onion, garlic, and jalapeño and puree until fairly smooth. Season to taste.

Return to pot over medium heat and boil the salsa about 15 minutes or until desired consistency is acquired (it should be neither too thin nor too thick). Store in refrigerator until ready to use; it will keep for nearly a week.

Avocado Sauce

(MAKES 1 PINT)

3 medium ripe avocados, peeled, pitted, and chopped
½ pound fresh jalapeños, destemmed, deseeded, and chopped
2 ounces (about 20 cloves) garlic, chopped
1 bunch cilantro, chopped
1 cup 2% milk
Water as needed
Salt and pepper to taste

Place all ingredients except salt and pepper in a food processor and blend with as much water as necessary to achieve a smooth sauce. Season to taste. Store in refrigerator until ready to use; the sauce will keep for about 12 hours.

Orange Salsa

(MAKES 1 PINT)

1 tablespoon vegetable oil
1 pound dried *chiles de arbol,* destemmed, deseeded, and chopped
1 pound white onion, chopped
5 cloves garlic, chopped
2 cups water
Salt and pepper

Heat oil in a pan over a medium-high burner and fry chiles, onion, and garlic until golden. Remove from pan, transfer to a food processor, add water, and puree. Season to taste. Store the salsa in the refrigerator until ready to use; it will keep for a few days.

Salsa Roja

(MAKES 1 PINT)

1 pound dried *chiles de arbol,* destemmed, deseeded, and chopped
6 medium tomatillos, skins removed, chopped
4 ounces (about ½ medium) white onion, chopped
6 cloves garlic, chopped
2 cups water
Salt and pepper to taste

In a dry, shallow pan or on a griddle, toast chiles, tomatillos, onion, and garlic for 10 minutes. Remove from pan, transfer to a food processor, add water, and puree. Add salt and pepper to taste. Refrigerate the salsa until ready to use; it will keep for about a week.

Lou's Food Bar

1851 West 38th Avenue
Denver, CO 80211
(303) 458-0336
LOUSFOODBAR.COM
Chefs/Owners: Frank Bonanno and Mike Peshek

Frank Bonanno is not only one of Denver's most beloved and prolific chef-restaurateurs, he's also quite the wordsmith. While I could describe his Sunnyside homage to Americana in my own words—low-key, down-home, and neighborly, yet smart and snappy, too—I'd just as soon quote him at delightful length:

"When you travel through Europe, some of the best restaurants are just off the highways and alongside rail stations. They're nondescript, age-worn venues—no tablecloths or elaborate decor—where you might find the owner serving wine made from grapes grown on the hillside out back or hand-rolled pastas on a menu that covers an unexpectedly wide geographic range. Before the fast-food revolution of the 1950s, it was that way in America as well. We had a culture of old roadside diners—the kinds of places where pies rest in a countertop display case, the specialties include everything from

smothered burritos to meat loaf to gyros, and breakfast is served all day. I love those diners in Europe, and I love them here—they're a testament to cultural diversity and to the foods in which we find solace.

"I wanted Lou's to be that place, recalling a time when farms were family run and everyone had an apple cellar—where all the food was comfort food and the bar was as long as the menu. A place where, if you came in two or three times, you would be remembered and warmly greeted—attended to and smiled upon. A place as comforting as a plate of fried chicken."

From the drinks served in Mason jars to the potted *rillettes du jour,* spaghetti and meatballs, and brunch-time coffee-cake french toast with espresso butter, Lou's is all that and then some.

BLACKENED FISH SANDWICH
WITH CELERY ROOT REMOULADE

According to chef Mike Peshek (pictured on page 122), the ingredients for this sandwich can be easily doubled or quadrupled to serve two or four; you should not need to make extra remoulade.

(SERVES 1)

For the remoulade:

2 whole cloves raw garlic plus 1 tablespoon chopped
    garlic, sautéed in small amount of vegetable oil
2 egg yolks
Salt and pepper to taste
1¾ cups light cooking oil
¼ cup plus 1 tablespoon lemon juice
1 celery root, diced

For the seasoning:

1 tablespoon sweet paprika
1½ teaspoons salt
1 teaspoon cayenne pepper
1 teaspoon onion powder
1 teaspoon garlic powder
¾ teaspoon black pepper
¾ teaspoon white pepper
½ teaspoon dried thyme
½ teaspoon dried oregano

Blended cooking oil as required
1 (6-ounce) piece mahimahi
1 french roll
Butter to taste
2 slices fresh tomato
2 slices red onion
1 leaf butter lettuce

Place whole garlic into a food processor and puree, wiping down the sides of the container two or three times to ensure the mince is uniform. Add the egg yolks, salt, and pepper and puree until incorporated. While the motor is running, slowly add the oil until you have a thick aioli, wiping down the sides as necessary. Slowly add ¼ cup lemon juice to thin out the mixture; check and adjust the seasoning. Fold the celery root, chopped garlic, and remaining lemon juice into 1 cup aioli and refrigerate. (Can be made up to 3 days in advance, with any leftovers used in other dips or spreads.)

To make the seasoning, thoroughly combine all ingredients in a good-size bowl.

Coat the bottom of a medium-size pan with blended oil and place over high heat. Dredge the fish in the seasoning to coat, add to the hot pan, and sear on both sides until cooked through; a few minutes should do it. While the fish is cooking, split and lightly toast the french roll, then spread butter and remoulade on both halves.

Place the fish on the bottom half of the roll; layer with the tomato, onion, and lettuce, and add the top of the roll.

Masterpiece Delicatessen

1575 Central Street
Denver, CO 80211
(303) 561-3354
MASTERPIECEDELI.COM
Chef/Co-Owner: Justin Brunson; Co-Owner: Steve Allee

At first glance, nothing about this mod LoHi joint quite makes sense. The high-ceilinged space boasts more wall than floor footage, and patio seating surpasses that of the interior, where all of six tables are barely supplemented by a window-side counter. Hues of wincingly bright lemon curd and chocolate would better suit a cupcakery than a deli. Yet capacity crowds go to show that the quality of the grub, at least, is crystal clear to everyone.

As jolly, red-bearded top toque Justin Brunson sees it, "Chefs love to eat sandwiches, but when we opened, there was no place in town that was essentially offering a fine-dining experience between two slices of bread, to paraphrase my partner. It seemed like a no-brainer to us to open up a cool, laid-back place where every sandwich, across the board, would be amazing as well as affordable." They start, of course, with lovingly tended and scrupulously procured ingredients: slow-roasted pork shoulder and twelve-hour brisket, sautéed wild mushrooms and fresh pears, artisanal salami and house-made condiments. Atop such building blocks, says Brunson, "I let the boys on the line play with whatever they want." Daily specials might incorporate foie gras or herb-roasted chicken; today's Iowa-style breaded pork tenderloin on a bun may be tomorrow's leg-of-lamb Reuben with sauerkraut and swiss cheese on toasted rye. What's more, Masterpiece is the rare sandwich counter with a full liquor license: that hot pastrami or Italian sub goes down all the easier with a Colorado microbrew or old-school cocktail (think screwdrivers, mojitos, and vodka tonics).

Mind you, Brunson's ambitions go far beyond the hand-held entrees on which

he hopes to build "a bar-and-grill concept at some point." A few blocks away from the deli stands Old Major, which opened to clamorous acclaim in early 2013; "seafood, swine, and wine is our tagline," says the chef (who also owns the Denver Bacon Company) of the white-hot spot, where creations like pork–matzoh ball soup and truffled pistachio sausage over escargot vinaigrette reveal skill commensurate with the kitchen's chutzpah. Still, it's nice to know that when the humble need for comfort trumps the loftier desire to challenge your palate, this sandwich shop will still deliver in spades.

Seared Ahi Tuna Sandwich

The chili pepper–based Japanese spice mixture known as *shichimi togarashi* is a staple at Asian markets—and the equivalent of a not-so-secret handshake among local chefs.

(SERVES 4)

For the Asian slaw:

3 cups julienned napa cabbage

¼ cup shredded carrot

1½ cups rice wine vinegar

1½ cups water

1 tablespoon white sugar

1 teaspoon salt

¼ cup mayonnaise

2 tablespoons shallots, minced

1 teaspoon prepared wasabi

Salt to taste

4 large English muffins

4 (4-ounce) pieces of sushi-grade ahi tuna

Freshly ground black pepper to taste

4 tablespoons *shichimi togarashi*

About 2 teaspoons canola oil

To make the slaw, mix all ingredients together and store in a glass container. (Keeps for 10 days in the refrigerator; use leftovers as a side dish.)

Mix mayonnaise, shallots, and wasabi in a small bowl and season with salt to taste. Set aside. Toast the English muffins.

Season tuna steaks with salt, black pepper, and *togarashi* and place in a large, cast-iron skillet with 2 teaspoons oil (or just enough oil to coat the bottom) over medium-high heat. Sear fish for about 1 minute on each side. Cut each piece into 5 slices with a sharp knife.

Smear each toasted English-muffin half with wasabi mayo. Lay 5 slices tuna on each of the 4 bottom halves. Squeeze excess liquid from the slaw and place a healthy spoonful atop the tuna. Place the muffin tops on the sandwiches and enjoy!

White-Truffled Egg Salad Sandwich

(SERVES 4)

8 farm-fresh eggs
¼ cup mayonnaise
½ small red onion, diced
1 tablespoon capers, rinsed
1½ teaspoons white truffle oil
Salt and freshly ground black pepper to taste
2 tablespoons good-quality butter
8 slices good-quality country white bread
4 leaves romaine lettuce, washed and dried fully

Place eggs in saucepan, cover with cold water, and bring to a boil. Shut off the heat and let sit for 12 minutes, then shock with ice water until cool enough to peel under running water.

Roughly mash the eggs in a nonreactive (preferably ceramic) bowl with mayonnaise, red onion, capers, and truffle oil; season with salt and pepper.

In a large sauté pan, melt butter on medium heat and toast bread until golden brown. Divide the egg salad evenly among four pieces of toast; top with romaine and the remaining toast slices and serve.

Foie Gras with Pear-Apple Compote, Côteaux du Layon Gelée, Port-Balsamic Reduction & Brioche

Former executive chef Thanawat Bates, who's since moved on to Las Vegas, provided the following recipes. Though there will be some of compote left over, Bates advises making a full batch; it will keep refrigerated for a couple of weeks and would go well with pork chops or buttermilk pancakes. The balsamic reduction will keep, refrigerated in a squeeze bottle, for at least a month.

Ask a reputable butcher, such as Oliver's Meat & Seafood Market in Denver's Country Club neighborhood (1718 East 6th Avenue, Denver; 303-733-4629; oliversmeatmarketllc .com), about acquiring the foie lobes, or you can obtain them directly through Hudson Valley at hudsonvalleyfoiegras.com. Côteaux du Layon is a Chenin Blanc–based dessert wine from the Loire Valley, which you can order from a fine wine shop like Mondo Vino (3601 West 32nd Avenue, Denver; 303-458-3858; mondovino.net) in Highlands Square, where you'll also find cassis, a blackcurrant liqueur. Your favorite gourmet retailer should carry Banyuls vinegar—made from yet another sweet French wine—or know where you can find it.

(SERVES 6)

For the compote:

½ cup honey
¼ cup apple cider vinegar
¼ cup Banyuls vinegar
2 tablespoons apple cider
2 tablespoons cassis
3 Granny Smith apples
2 Bosc pears
Salt and pepper to taste

For the gelée:

4 sheets silver-strength gelatin
100 milliliters Côteaux du Layon (⅕ of a 500-milliliter bottle)

For the reduction:

4 cups plus 1 tablespoon balsamic vinegar
2 cups Port wine
2 cups apple juice

5 cups basil
½ cup olive oil
1 Grade A lobe Hudson Valley foie gras, cut into 6 pieces about 2½ ounces each
Kosher salt and cracked black pepper to taste
6 (3 x 1-inch) rectangles cut from purchased brioche, buttered and toasted
½ cup microgreens

Special equipment:

16-ounce squeeze bottle

First, make the compote: Combine honey, vinegars, cider, and cassis in a nonreactive saucepan and cook over medium-high heat until the mixture is reduced to a light syrup, 8–10 minutes.

Peel and core the apples and pears and dice the flesh small. Add the fruit to the syrup, season to taste with salt and pepper, and cook, stirring

frequently, until the fruit is tender and the liquid has been absorbed, about 25 minutes. Let cool and refrigerate in a shallow baking dish until ready to use.

To make the gelée: Soak (bloom) the gelatin in a bowl with ice water for 5–10 minutes. Meanwhile, warm the wine in a nonreactive saucepan over low heat for about 5 minutes, then remove pan from stove. Squeeze excess water from softened gelatin and add to wine. Once dissolved, pour the mixture into a clean sheet pan and let set for 1 hour, then cut into ½- to 1-inch squares.

While the gelée is setting, make the reduction: Heat a large saucepan to medium, add 4 cups balsamic vinegar, the Port, and the apple juice and simmer until 1½–2 cups are left and the reduction coats the back of a spoon. Remove from heat and stir in remaining tablespoon balsamic vinegar. Let cool and store in squeeze bottle.

Preheat the oven to 350°F. Prepare an ice bath, bring a good-size pot of lightly salted water to a boil, and blanch the basil in the pot for 30 seconds. Shock the leaves in the ice bath, drain, and squeeze out excess water; then transfer to a food processor with the olive oil and blend until smooth. Next, heat a heavy (preferably cast-iron) pan over a medium-high burner. Season foie pieces with salt and pepper and sear in the pan for 2–3 minutes on each side; place them on a sheet pan and finish in the oven for 3 minutes. (This method, says Bates, will ensure that "they have three textures: crispy on the outside, warm on the inside, and cool in the center.")

On each of six serving plates, add a piece of brioche and top it with a piece of foie, a small mound of compote, and a pinch of microgreens, in that order. Arrange a few cubes of gelée and another dollop or two of compote around the brioche; finally, drizzle the plates with balsamic reduction and basil oil and serve.

Artichoke Soup with "Ham-and-Cheese" Sandwiches

As served at the restaurant, this soup is enriched with *barigoule,* a sort of artichoke stew from Provence; what follows is a simplified version. It will actually yield more than you need (enough for about six people); you may simply increase the sandwich ingredients accordingly or freeze the leftovers, which will keep for about a month.

Spain's famed *jamón ibérico*—long-cured ham from the *pata negra,* a black-footed, free-roaming pig breed sometimes raised on acorns—is the pride of many a gourmet meat-and-cheese counter. But if it's too rich for your blood (or rather your budget), you can use Italian prosciutto as a substitute.

(SERVES 4)

For the white anchovy aioli:

½ clove garlic
1 jumbo egg yolk
2 white anchovy fillets
1 regular anchovy fillet
1 tablespoon Dijon mustard

Juice of 1 lemon
1 tablespoon ice water
5 tablespoons extra-virgin olive oil
¼ cup grapeseed oil
¼ cup sour cream
Kosher salt and freshly ground black pepper to taste

For the soup (yields about 2–2½ quarts):

12 tablespoons whole unsalted butter, divided

2 cups thoroughly cleaned and large-diced leek,
   white part only

1 pound frozen artichoke hearts

1 quart heavy cream

3 cloves garlic, peeled and mashed

¼ cup dry white wine

4 quarts chicken stock

1 cup crème fraîche

2 teaspoons fresh thyme

Lemon juice to taste

Salt and pepper to taste

For the sandwiches:

Butter as needed

8 slices brioche

8 slices *jamón ibérico* or prosciutto

8 slices fontina cheese

For garnish:

½ preserved lemon, julienned (available at specialty
   gourmet shops)

3–4 teaspoons microparsley

For the aioli: Place the garlic, yolk, anchovies, mustard, lemon juice, and ice water in a food processor and blend. With the motor running, add the olive and grapeseed oils in a slow, steady stream until the aioli emulsifies. Fold in sour cream and season with salt and pepper to taste; set aside.

To make the soup: Place a large stew pot over high heat. Add 9 tablespoons butter and sauté the leek and artichoke hearts until softened, 30–40 minutes. Meanwhile, in a separate pot, bring the heavy cream to a simmer with the garlic and reduce by half (this too should take about 30 minutes). Strain, discarding the garlic, and set aside.

Deglaze the artichoke-leek mixture with white wine until almost evaporated. Add stock and continue to cook over medium heat for 45–60 minutes, then add the reduced cream and cook for another 10–15 minutes. Carefully stir in the crème fraîche and thyme; season with salt and pepper. Transfer the soup to a food processor and puree (in batches as necessary); with the motor running, slowly add lemon juice and the remaining 3 tablespoons butter. Adjust the seasoning to taste.

For the sandwiches: Butter each slice of brioche on one side. Layer 2 pieces ham and cheese each on the unbuttered sides of 4 of the slices; top with the remaining 4 slices, butter side up. Heat a pan or griddle over a medium burner; then toast the sandwiches for approximately 3 minutes per side. Remove crusts and cut in half (depending on the size of the bread slices).

In a small mixing bowl, combine the preserved lemon and parsley. Ladle soup into four bowls and serve the sandwiches on the side, topped with a dollop of aioli (you may have some left over) and a little of the parsley mixture. Serve immediately.

Panzano

Hotel Monaco
909 17th Street
Denver, CO 80202
(303) 296-3525
panzano-denver.com
Owner: Kimpton Hotels & Restaurants; Chef: Elise Wiggins

In the past decade, Colorado's culinary cup hath runneth over with admirable, inspirational, influential chefs. But few may be quite so simply beloved as the vivacious Elise Wiggins, whose personality isn't merely reflected in her cooking—it fills the room all the way from the kitchen. As longtime top toque at Panzano, she makes the sprawling, buzzing downtown-hotel restaurant feel like a cozy second home.

It's partly that her passion for contemporary Italian food is matched by her compassion for others. She sources mostly organic ingredients, largely from local purveyors (indeed, sustainable practices inform the entire operation, from the recycling

program to the cleaning regimen). Her gluten-free selections are nearly as wide as the regular menus, including pizza and sandwiches. And her style is practically collaborative: "I've evolved with my guests, who have been instrumental to our success," she reflects. "When trying out new recipes, I rely heavily on their feedback. If they aren't absolutely crazy about a dish that I run as a special, then it doesn't go on the menu."

In that light, the best seats in the house may be at the chef's counter, where you're privy to all manner of off-menu tidbits. But it's no less a pleasure just to soak up the atmosphere in the handsome dining room decked out in rich tones of oyster and cranberry, catching snippets of shop talk from the movers and shakers over their power breakfasts and business lunches, or watching the dolled-up theatergoers stream in come dinnertime. Then again, the bar on the other side of the in-house bakery is a prime gathering spot during a happy hour that lasts all afternoon; veteran GM Josh Mayo graciously presides, sleek iPad wine list in hand.

Wherever you sit, you'll be treated to baskets of warm focaccia alongside lusty pastas like gnocchi with rabbit confit and Gorgonzola. To plump, pancetta-wrapped shrimp stuffed with dates and arranged over creamy polenta. To chocolate-cherry shortbread topped with crème fraîche gelato and capped off, perhaps, with a spot of chamomile grappa. And, throughout it all, to the warmth that emanates from "foodies serving foodies," as Wiggins puts it. Home is where the heartiness is.

Rosemary Tagliatelle with Lemon Emulsion, Cranberries & Pine Nuts

(SERVES 4)

For the pasta:

1 egg

¾ teaspoon salt

⅓–½ cup water, plus extra as needed

1 cup all-purpose flour, plus extra for dusting

1 cup semolina

¼ cup finely chopped fresh rosemary

For the lemon emulsion:

1 tablespoon olive oil

2 garlic cloves, peeled and chopped

1 fresh shallot, diced small

½ cup white wine

½ cup chicken stock

Juice and zest of 1 small lemon

4 tablespoons unsalted butter, cold

Salt to taste

1 tablespoon unsalted butter

4 tablespoons dried cranberries

4 tablespoons toasted pine nuts

Salt to taste

4 tablespoons goat cheese, preferably from
   a local creamery

4 tablespoons microbasil

Special equipment:

rolling pin

pasta machine (optional)

To make the pasta: Lightly beat the egg with the salt in a small bowl; add ¼ cup water and mix just to combine.

Sift the flour and semolina into a large bowl; stir in rosemary. Make a well in the middle of the flour and add the egg mixture; mix to incorporate. Add as much of the remaining water as necessary to form a dough. (If it's still too dry, add a little more.)

Form the dough into a ball and knead for about 5 minutes, or until smooth and workable. Cover and let rest for 30 minutes, then turn out onto a lightly floured surface. With a rolling pin, roll out until thin, cut into workable pieces as necessary, and use your pin or pasta machine to roll into very thin sheets. Cut into strips about 12 inches long and ⅛-inch wide. Cover and set aside.

For the lemon emulsion: Heat saucepan with oil over a medium-high burner. Add garlic and shallot; gently cook until the latter is translucent but not brown. Add wine, stock, and lemon juice; simmer for 5 minutes. Pour the mixture into a blender, add lemon zest, and liquefy ingredients; with the motor still running, add butter a

tablespoon at a time, then salt, and continue blending for 1 minute. Adjust seasoning to taste.

In a pot of salted boiling water, cook pasta until al dente and drain immediately. Melt 1 tablespoon butter in a warm sauté pan; add cranberries, pine nuts, and finally pasta. Toss quickly to combine and season to taste with salt.

Place approximately 4 liquid ounces or ½ cup lemon emulsion in each of four serving bowls; evenly divide pasta among them. Garnish with an equal amount of goat cheese and microbasil.

FRIED BRUSSELS SPROUTS WITH CIDER REDUCTION & ROSEMARY PISTACHIOS

(SERVES 4)

1 tablespoon finely chopped fresh rosemary leaves

1 tablespoon kosher salt

2½ cups apple cider

½ cup shelled pistachios

Vegetable oil as directed

26 brussels sprouts, trimmed and halved

1 tart apple, such as Granny Smith, grated with skin on

Special equipment:

frying thermometer

Thoroughly combine rosemary and salt in a small bowl; set aside. In a small, nonreactive sauté pan over high heat, boil cider until it is reduced to a thin syrup, about 5–10 minutes (you will have about ¼ cup). Set aside in a nonreactive dish to cool. Add pistachios to pan and toast (be careful not to burn). Remove the nuts, chop them coarsely by hand or in a food processor, and combine them in a large bowl with rosemary salt to taste. Set aside.

In a large, heavy pot, heat enough oil to cover the brussels sprouts to 350°F and fry the sprouts until the outside leaves begin to turn golden brown. (Do not overfry, or they will become mushy.) Remove the sprouts from the oil and toss them together with the pistachio mixture.

To serve, divide sprouts evenly among four plates, liberally drizzle with the reduced apple cider, and top each with grated apple.

Parallel Seventeen

1600 East 17th Avenue
Denver, CO 80218
(303) 399-0988
PARALLELSEVENTEEN.COM
Chef/Owner: Mary Nguyen

Technically, the name alludes to real-world map coordinates—the latitude of the post-Geneva demarcation between North and South Vietnam. But upon entering, one suspects that it actually marks some imaginary space in which the bright and breezy beaches of old Indochina somehow border the sleekest cityscapes of today, as brick walls, exposed beams, and brushed metal juxtapose banana-leaf bouquets and sculptures dangling like so much coastal flotsam: the skeletons of windswept umbrellas,

chunks of seeming coral reef. Here, East and West, tradition and novelty blend seamlessly, dreamily. Chef Mary Nguyen fills dumplings with white asparagus and bathes them in red curry bisque; tosses fresh pappardelle with chrysanthemum buds; updates classic salade Niçoise with five-spice duck confit and miso vinaigrette; even slathers Southern-fried chicken and waffles in Thai chili butter—and pairs it all with, say, Spanish wine as well as sake.

More than anything, however, this Uptown corner haunt is grounded in the community immediately surrounding the intersection of Franklin Street and 17th Avenue (to which its name of course also refers). "In an industry that's constantly changing," muses Nguyen, "I'm proud that I've been able to create a 'family' of longtime staff and regulars who've been coming in since the day we opened." In their honor, she aims to "give back as much as possible" through monthly "Dine Out for a Cause" nights to support local nonprofits, half-price deals on wine every Tuesday, and the like; a recently added heated patio invites passersby to kick back al fresco nearly year round. Parallel Seventeen is thus, above all, a friendly neighborhood joint—minus the poppers and PBR, plus the potstickers and rice ale.

Ginger-and-Coconut Encrusted Calamari with Sweet Chili Sauce

Says Nguyen, "The idea here is to get small pieces of all the ingredients together in one bite to experience the balance of five flavors: bitter, spicy, sour, sweet, and salty." Serve the extra sauce—which will keep, refrigerated, for a couple of weeks—with dumplings or egg rolls, or you can reduce the measurements by half if preferred.

(SERVES 2 AS AN APPETIZER)

For the sauce (yields about 4 cups):

2 tablespoons cornstarch

¼ cup plus 2 cups water

2 tablespoons soybean oil

2 tablespoons minced ginger

2 tablespoons minced garlic

2 bird (Thai) chilies, finely minced

½ cup sake

½ cup fish sauce

¾ cup white vinegar

½ cup *sambal oelek* (an Indonesian chili paste available at Asian markets)

¾ cup brown sugar

3 quarts canola oil

8 ounces calamari tentacles and tubes, cut into ¼-inch rings

2 ounces calamari steak, cut into 1-inch strips

2 very thin slices whole lemon

2 very thin slices whole orange

6–8 thin slices jalapeño

1 tablespoon minced ginger

½ red pear, cored, seeded, and julienned

2 cups watercress, cleaned and trimmed

6 ounces packaged tempura batter

2 cups fine panko bread crumbs

Heaping ½ cup unsweetened coconut flakes

1 teaspoon kosher salt

Special equipment:

deep-fat fryer and/or frying thermometer

To make the chili sauce: Add cornstarch and ¼ cup water to a small mixing bowl; whisk to combine well. Set aside. Heat soybean oil in a heavy, nonreactive saucepan over medium-high heat. Add ginger, garlic, and chilies and sauté until aromatic, 2–3 minutes. Add the sake; allow the alcohol to burn off, about 5 minutes, and then add the rest of the ingredients, including the remaining 2 cups water. Bring to a boil. Slowly add the cornstarch slurry, whisking well, until the sauce thickens, about 5 minutes. Remove from heat and let cool.

Start the calamari by heating canola oil in a large, heavy pot or a deep fryer to 350°F (check with thermometer).

Combine the calamari pieces, lemon, orange, jalapeño, and ginger in a bowl; set aside. In another large mixing bowl, combine the pear and watercress and set aside.

In a third bowl, prepare the tempura batter according to package instructions; finally, in a fourth bowl, make the breading by combining the panko crumbs, coconut, and salt. Coat the calamari pieces and the orange, lemon, and jalapeño slices in the tempura batter, then dredge in the breading. Carefully add the sliced citrus and jalapeño slices to the pot or fryer and cook until golden (about 2 minutes), turning once or twice. Remove with a slotted spoon and drain on paper towels. Next, add the calamari pieces, taking care not to overcrowd them

(they should be completely submerged in the oil, so divide into batches as necessary). Fry until golden (about 1–2 minutes), turning once. Remove with your slotted spoon and drain on paper towels.

Once drained, immediately toss the fried calamari, citrus slices, and jalapeños into the bowl with the watercress and pears; toss to slightly wilt the greens. Divide evenly between two serving plates and enjoy with dipping sauce on the side.

PHAT THAI

PHATTHAI.COM
CHEF/OWNER: MARK FISCHER

When Mark Fischer opened a Cherry Creek outpost of his Carbondale smash hit Phat Thai, he'd tell anyone within earshot that it wasn't "necessarily a Thai restaurant. Yes, I've been lucky enough to spend a lot of time traveling in Thailand, Malaysia, and Vietnam, and I developed an inherent curiosity about the food." But his very respect for the culinary traditions of Southeast Asia precluded any claims to "authenticity"—a fundamentally vexed concept in any case—and so his interest lay not in the stringent duplication of any particular dish but in the opportunity for alchemy it inspired.

Certainly the ultra-mod aspect of the two-story dining room pointed toward Fischer's intentions: papaya and curry hues popped, sweeping planes of chrome and glass gleamed, and the overall effect was one of some airy, faraway spice bazaar as viewed through a postindustrial prism. Of course, the menu only boosted the mood, putting as it did a chefly spin on homespun hawker-stall staples—be it the use of peanut brittle as a garnish for tofu and Chinese broccoli in peppered oyster sauce; haute duck- and crab-filled egg rolls; or the East-West savor of a salad combining green papaya, cashews, and coconut with roasted beets and grapefruit. A tray of seasonings on every table—red pepper flakes, fish sauce, sugar, and infused vinegar—allowed you to adjust the balance among heat, salt, sweetness, and acidity to taste. Of course, the kicky cocktails skewed exotic, too, spiked with ginger, lemongrass, chilies, and the like.

At press time, however, Fischer announced that he was closing Phat Thai to make way for Harman's Eat and Drink, a contemporary American concept based on his acclaimed Glenwood Springs property The Pullman. He does plan to reopen the Asian eatery elsewhere in Denver, but the new location has yet to be determined. Until then, may the following recipes tide you over.

Caramel Pork Belly with Watermelon Pickle & Thai Basil Salad

You will need at least a day to complete this recipe, which yields lots of extras. The watermelon pickle will keep for at least three months under refrigeration—in fact, says Fischer, "it only improves with age"—and the leftover vinaigrette should be used within three days; further storage details are provided below.

Ketjap manis is a sweet soy sauce from Indonesia that you should be able to find, along with several other ingredients listed here, at most Asian groceries.

(SERVES 8)

For the watermelon pickle:

1 (5-pound) watermelon
2 cups rice wine vinegar
3 shallots, thinly sliced
2 bird (Thai) chilies, thinly sliced
2 Kaffir lime leaves
2-inch piece of fresh ginger, peeled and sliced
2 tablespoons palm sugar
1 tablespoon kosher salt

For the master stock:

4 cloves garlic, smashed
6 white peppercorns
½ cup Chinese rice wine or cooking sherry
½ gallon (8 cups) chicken stock
¼ cup yellow bean paste
¼ cup ketjap manis
¼ cup oyster sauce
2-inch piece of ginger, washed and sliced thinly
1 cinnamon stick
2 pieces star anise

For the pork:

2 pounds pork belly
Canola or peanut oil as directed
½ cup blended oil

For the caramel sauce:

8 ounces palm or light brown sugar
½ cup water
1 cinnamon stick
1 piece star anise

For the Thai basil salad:

½ cup fresh lime juice
¼ cup blended oil
¼ cup good-quality fish sauce
¼ cup water
½ cup green onion, trimmed and chopped coarsely
1 small bunch cilantro, stems on, chopped
½ cup mint leaves, stems on, chopped coarsely
2 bird (Thai) chilies, destemmed and roughly chopped
2 cups Thai basil leaves, trimmed

For the garnish:

½ cup thinly sliced shallots, fried in ½ cup peanut or
    canola oil until crisp

Begin with the watermelon pickle: Using a sturdy knife, cut the melon into manageable wedges so you can remove the rind. Cut away and discard the green peel, then cut the remaining rind into pieces approximately 1-inch square. Dice enough of the melon itself to yield 2 cups and chill, covered, until ready to complete the recipe (use the rest as desired).

Over high heat, bring a large pot of salted water to a boil. Add the rind, return to a boil, and cook until tender. Transfer to a good-size, nonreactive container. Meanwhile, prepare the brine by placing the remaining ingredients in a pot over medium heat and bringing them to a simmer. Remove from stove and pour the hot liquid over the rind. Refrigerate, covered, for at least 24 hours.

When the pickle is ready, make the stock: Using a mortar and pestle or in a food processor, mash or puree garlic and peppercorns into a paste. In a large stockpot over medium-high heat, sauté the paste until fragrant, stirring frequently, about 1–2 minutes. Add the rice wine or sherry and stir to deglaze. Add the remaining ingredients and bring to a simmer; cook, skimming the surface as necessary, 30 minutes. Strain into a nonreactive container and reserve.

To prepare the pork: Cut the pork belly into manageable pieces, about 6 inches in diameter. Pour canola or peanut oil to a depth of 1 inch into a sturdy, good-size pot over high heat; once bubbling, add pork and fry until golden brown, about 1 minute. Drain on absorbent paper towels.

Preheat the oven to 325°F. Transfer pork to a lidded, ovenproof saucepan large enough to accommodate it snugly. Add prepared stock to cover the pork (the remainder, if any, will keep frozen for a couple of months), place on the stovetop over medium heat, and bring to a

simmer. Cover the pot and braise in the oven about 2 hours, or until the meat is very tender.

Remove belly pieces from stock and allow to cool slightly; wrap each in plastic wrap and set aside. Strain the stock into a separate container (you will need 2 cups to complete the recipe) and set aside.

To make the caramel sauce: Place sugar and water in a large pot over medium-low heat. As the sugar dissolves and begins to lightly caramelize, add the cinnamon and star anise and continue to cook until the mixture is dark amber, about 30 minutes. Carefully add the reserved 2 cups stock, increase the heat to medium-high, and simmer until the mixture thickens slightly, about 5 minutes. The resulting sauce should taste both sweet and salty. Strain and reserve.

Prepare the vinaigrette for the salad by placing all ingredients except Thai basil in a blender and pulsing until smooth. Set aside.

To complete the dish, cut braised pork belly into 1-inch cubes to yield 4 cups (any remaining meat will freeze well). Bring ½ cup blended oil to a bubble in a large pan over high heat; lower to medium and sauté the cubed pork until crisp, about 1 minute. Drain well and discard the oil, leaving the meat in the pan. Add 1 cup of caramel sauce (there may be some left over) and reduce until the sauce has a rich texture and just coats the meat, about 1 more minute.

Transfer the cubed pork belly to a serving platter and arrange as desired, along with 1 cup pickled rind and the reserved, diced watermelon. Place the Thai basil in a bowl and toss to combine with a small amount of the vinaigrette (about 2 tablespoons), then arrange it around the platter. Garnish with crisp shallots and serve.

Blueberry Lemonade

To infuse the vinegar, you will need at least two weeks; once ready, it will keep indefinitely for use in cocktails, salad dressings, and so on. (See glossary regarding simple syrup.)

(SERVES 1)

For the blueberry vinegar:

1 pound blueberries
1 liter distilled white vinegar
Granulated sugar as directed

2 lemon wedges
2 fluid ounces Hangar 1 Maine Wild Blueberry Vodka
½ fluid ounce simple syrup
Splash of seltzer

Special equipment:

cocktail shaker

Macerate the fruit by submerging it in vinegar in a nonreactive container; cover and let infuse for 14 days.

Strain fruit from vinegar and discard. Measure the remaining infused liquid by volume. Add an equal amount by volume of granulated sugar, place in a nonreactive pot, and bring to a boil. Reduce heat and simmer 10 minutes.

Remove from heat and strain once more into a nonreactive container. Refrigerate for a couple of hours or until chilled; reserve ¾ fluid ounce (about 1½ tablespoons) for the cocktail, and store the remainder in glass, refrigerated, for future use.

In the pint glass of a cocktail shaker, muddle the lemon well. Fill with ice. Add vodka, reserved vinegar, and simple syrup and shake well. Pour into a highball glass and top with seltzer.

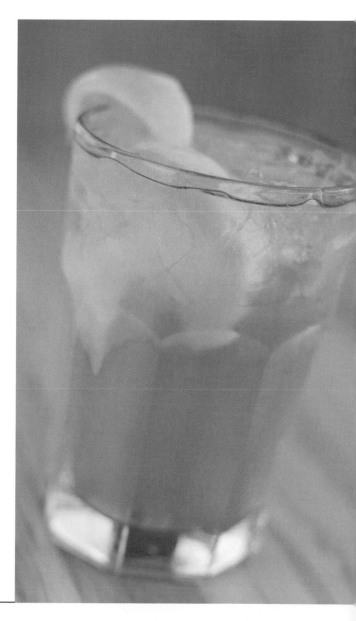

Pizzeria Locale

1730 Pearl Street
Boulder, CO 80301
(720) 708-2244

550 Broadway Unit C
Denver, CO 80203
(720) 508-8828
PIZZERIALOCALE.COM
Owners: Bobby Stuckey and Lachlan Mackinnon-Patterson; Chef: Jordan Wallace

From the day they opened the restaurant that, few would deny, first brought Colorado to the sustained attention of the national food media—Frasca Food and Wine (page 68)— Bobby Stuckey and Lachlan Mackinnon-Patterson have been applying their singular talents toward the pursuit of, not to mince words, gastronomic perfection. The move to open a pizzeria adjacent to their Boulder flagship in 2011 was no detour.

Artisanship is paramount here. The tiled beehive oven famously hand-built by Campanian craftsman Stefano Ferrara, the prosciutto slicer custom-assembled in Friuli, and Dave Woody's large-scale photographs of archetypal Neapolitan street scenes all reflect the owners' reverence for the cultural context in which one of the world's most beloved foodstuffs originated as much as for the culinary nuts and bolts from which it's constructed: the puffed yet crackling crust, the San Marzano tomato sauce, the imported or house-made cheeses. Their wholehearted immersion into the realm of the *pizzaiolo* precipitates your own; whether taking a classic *aperitivo* with tuna-stuffed peppers or a glass of Aglianico alongside a pie whose integrity inheres in its utter simplicity or even just a quick espresso *corretto,* you'll feel about as close in spirit to the Italians depicted on the walls, going about their daily business, as you ever will stateside.

Now Denver's getting a slice of the action: at the time of this writing, Stuckey and Mackinnon-Patterson had just opened an outpost in the trendy Baker District. Leave it to them to find the ideal, well, locale.

INSALATA ARTIGIANALE

(SERVES 4)

¼ cup grapeseed or other neutral oil

¼ cup olive oil

3 tablespoons red wine vinegar

Chopped fresh oregano to taste

Salt and pepper to taste

1 romaine heart, trimmed and cleaned

½ head radicchio, trimmed and cleaned

¼ head green cabbage, trimmed and cleaned

½ small red onion

1 cup spicy salame, such as sopressata, cut into
    2-inch matchsticks

¾ cup provolone, cut into 2-inch matchsticks

½ cup drained canned chickpeas

In a small bowl, whisk together the oils and vinegar to emulsify; add the oregano, salt, and pepper, whisk to combine, and adjust seasonings to taste. Set aside.

Cut romaine and radicchio into bite-size pieces and place in a large bowl. Thinly slice the cabbage and onion and add to the bowl along with the salame, provolone, and chickpeas. Toss to combine. Add dressing to taste (there may be some left over), toss to lightly coat, and serve.

PUNCH BOWL SOCIAL FOOD & DRINK

65 BROADWAY
DENVER, CO 80203
(303) 765-2695
PUNCHBOWLSOCIAL.COM
OWNER: ROBERT THOMPSON
CHEF: SERGIO ROMERO

At nearly 25,000 square feet, this former overstock warehouse in the Baker District gave restaurateur Robert Thompson (pictured) more room to develop his concept for a one-stop party shop than he could ever possibly need. Or so you'd think. But the owner of Le Grand Bistro & Oyster Bar (page 114) has somehow managed to devote every last inch to one form of fun or another. Punch Bowl Social is an entertainment complex of the coolest, most eye-popping order.

The entire space is framed by two-story-high exposed ceilings, cement floors, and giant windows; at its vast, key-shaped center stands a bowling alley serviced by a circular bar below a chandelier made of antlers. On one side, a lounge evokes the library of some country manor as viewed through a psychedelic lens, with elaborate carved armchairs and couches arranged around an outsize, column-flanked fireplace beneath gilt-framed mirrors and the mounted plaster sculpture of an enormous deer's head. On the other side, a retro-toned diner, warmed by the glow of the open kitchen, already emits a well-worn, *Nighthawks*-esque aura. And in every other nook and cranny, there's something to grab your attention—a game of darts, shuffleboard, or foosball; kitschy oil paintings of fox hunts and snippets of graffiti; an entire video arcade, along with pinball machines and Ping-Pong and pool tables, on the turquoise-walled mezzanine.

Food and drink could easily have been lost in the shuffle (no pun intended). But Thompson, smart cookie that he is, has assembled a crackerjack bar and kitchen crew to ensure otherwise nearly 24/7. Designed by rising culinary star Sergio Romero, the menu's rife with

hash-house classics and blue-plate specials whose finishing touches skew gourmet. For breakfast, there's house-cured pastrami hash and duck confit–topped huevos rancheros; as the clock ticks on, cornmeal-fried okra with jalapeño-pear jelly, elk burgers, and herbed bison meatloaf come into play. Draft microbrews, keg wines, spiked milk shakes, and java concoctions supplement a list of craft cocktails that's centered, of course, on punches. In short, you could wander in 'round daybreak and stay past midnight wanting for nothing the entire time. We're not really suggesting you should—but you could. And you'd be welcome.

BAKED BEANS

Begin soaking the beans a day in advance, and reserve several hours of cooking time.

(SERVES 8)

1 pound dried white beans, such as Great
   Northern or navy
1 tablespoon vegetable oil
8 ounces pancetta, diced
1 yellow onion, diced
1 tablespoon minced garlic
3 cups vegetable stock
1 cup ketchup
½ cup brown sugar
¼ cup dark molasses
2 tablespoons Worcestershire sauce
2 teaspoons cayenne pepper
1 teaspoon ground mustard
1 sprig thyme
2 bay leaves
Salt to taste

Place beans in a large pot, cover with 2 inches
water, and soak overnight. Drain and set aside.

Preheat the oven to 250°F.

Place a large, heavy-bottomed, ovenproof pot
(preferably cast-iron) over medium heat. Add
oil and pancetta and cook until crispy, then add
the onion and garlic and cook until tender, 8–10
minutes, before adding the beans and remaining
ingredients (except salt). Cover and bake in
the oven for 8 hours or until beans are tender,
checking the liquid level a few hours in and
adding more water as necessary (they should be
just submerged; in the end, they shouldn't be too
soupy). Season with salt and enjoy.

DENVER'S SOULFUL SECRET

Native Denverite, ex-political analyst, and all-around mensch Adrian Miller is a culinary historian specializing in African-American foodways. His first book, titled *Soul Food: The Surprising Story of an American Cuisine, One Plate at a Time,* will be published in fall 2013.

"There are black people in Denver?" That's the usual response when I tell non-Coloradans where I'm from. "Absolutely!" I say, and explain that African Americans have lived—and operated restaurants—in the city since its earliest days as a mining and ranching town, most of them Southerners who can trace their roots to Arkansas and east Texas.

Denver's most soulful restaurant is CoraFaye's Café (2861 Colorado Boulevard; 303-333-5551). Amid the ambience of a grandmother's parlor room, diners can devour otherwise-scarce chitlins, pigs' feet, and rabbit as well as Southern standards like catfish, fried chicken, and collard greens, then wash it all down with a glass of red Kool-Aid. The coconut cake is among the best I've had.

It's also hard to beat Tom's Home Cookin' (800 East 26th Avenue; 303-388-8035), run by two white guys from Georgia in the heart of Five Points, a traditionally African-American neighborhood. This cash-only

weekday-lunch joint usually has a line forming by 11:30 a.m.; getting a table is like winning at Powerball—but you're really taking a gamble if you try to show up after 1 p.m. I love that they shout their daily menu into their voicemail, and that peach cobbler is considered a vegetable. How cool is that? In addition to the cobbler, I can't resist the crispy, well-seasoned catfish.

Denver's enjoying a barbecue renaissance of late. My current favorite is Boney's BBQ (1543 Champa Street; 303-825-9900; boneysbbq.com), tucked below street level steps away from the 16th Street Mall downtown. Though the proprietors are from Florida, the menu evokes the Deep South more than the Caribbean. The beef brisket, spareribs, and pulled pork all have the right mix of crunch, tenderness, and smoke that eludes me at so many other places—in fact, the omnipresent aroma of hickory can leave you smelling like bacon. You've been warned.

RACINES

650 SHERMAN STREET
DENVER, CO 80203
(303) 595-0418
RACINESRESTAURANT.COM
OWNERS: LEE GOODFRIEND AND DAVID RACINE; CHEF: MIKE ADAMS

Somewhere between the fern bars of yesteryear and the gastropubs of today sits Racines—a sprawling thirty-year-old institution with an equally giant menu yielding something for everyone morning, noon, and night. Gathered in the warm, woody, harvest-toned dining room centered around an island bar and flanked by a foliage-

fringed patio are regulars who, says co-owner Lee Goodfriend, "come every day. We get a lot of politicians working the room during breakfast and lunch; we get a lot of theater people who know that we're open relatively late, so they can get a meal after a performance without being rushed out. A tremendous number of families; a huge, great gay clientele. I love the diversity of this city."

This city, in turn, loves the diversity of the pickings. Early risers rev their engines over everything from house-made granola and bacon-speckled pancakes to huevos rancheros and buttermilk biscuits smothered in sausage gravy; no sooner are their dishes cleared than the kitchen starts turning out generous helpings of some seventy different dishes. Classic cobb salads and french onion soup. Vegetarian *báhn mì* and buffalo burgers. Batter-fried fish tacos and gooey eggplant Parmesan. Loaded potato skins, chicken-fried steak with mashed potatoes, and carrot cake or fruit cobbler for dessert. Given the labor required for such an array, you might expect to find some corners cut—but you'd be wrong. "We make everything from scratch. We roast our own turkey and beef. We make our own salad dressings and tortilla chips. The desserts are baked in house. These days, that sounds almost silly to say, but when we opened in 1983, not many places were doing that," Goodfriend points out.

What's more, even today, not many places bask in quite the earnest community glow Racines radiates. Regularly rotating artwork "gives us a change and helps local artists," she says. Flat-screen TVs placed discreetly along the bar welcome sports fans without distracting conversationalists. And seasonal displays— be it pumpkins carved by customers for Halloween or Christmas decorations—show holiday spirit in spades. Here's to another thirty.

Nutty Cheese Salad
with Honey-Mustard Dressing

The leftover dressing will keep, refrigerated, for a few days.

(SERVES 4)

For the dressing:

1 cup mayonnaise

6 tablespoons white wine vinegar

2 tablespoons prepared yellow mustard

1½ teaspoons finely diced onion

1½ teaspoons finely chopped parsley

1½ teaspoons confectioners' sugar

Pinch of salt

1½ cups canola oil

2 tablespoons plus 1 teaspoon honey

1 head romaine lettuce, washed and dried

8 ounces mixed field greens, washed and dried

4 ounces (1 cup) shredded fontina cheese

4 ounces (1 cup) shredded white cheddar

2 bananas, sliced into ¼-inch disks

16 grape tomatoes

1 avocado, cut into ¼-inch-thick slices

2 ounces (½ cup) hulled, roasted sunflower seeds

2 ounces (½ cup) roasted cashews

2 ounces (½ cup) roasted almonds, sliced

1 ounce (1 cup) puffed wheat, such as Arrowhead Mills
   (optional)

To make the dressing: Place all ingredients except the canola oil and honey in a food processor and blend to incorporate. Slowly add oil until well mixed; then add the honey slowly until thoroughly blended. Set aside.

Chop the romaine into bite-size pieces and toss to combine with the field greens, then transfer to four serving plates. Divide the remaining ingredients evenly among the plates in any arrangement you wish and dress with about 3–4 tablespoons per serving.

Row 14 Bistro & Wine Bar

891 14th Street
Denver, CO 80202
(303) 825-0100
row14denver.com
Owner: David Schneider

The materials are raw: reclaimed beetle kill. Steel wine-barrel rings. Bare cement. Carpet tiles. Yet the effect is anything but: From the burnished-gold chain-mail curtains lining the bar to the photographic mural in the black- and ochre-toned dining room that depicts a crowd of grinning French soccer fans circa 1940 passing a bottle of wine around, Row 14 is buffed to a high polish.

It's only fitting, then, that the kitchen sublimates all its funky street smarts in service of a worldly, coherent whole, defined by owner David Schneider as "American bistro fare with creative twists." While former chef Jensen Cummings, who provided the following recipes, set the vivid precedent via Asian-tinged creations like chicken-and-rabbit *rillettes* with rice wine mustard, the current kitchen crew takes a more Mediterranean tack, offering seared scallops over asparagus-risotto cakes in wild mushroom–bacon vinaigrette, for instance, or spaetzle with spaghetti squash, brussels sprouts, hazelnuts, and goat cheese fondue. And all those global accents find their echo in Schneider's diverse wine list, a compendium of some forty pours by the glass as well as sixty bottle selections—enough, he says, to cover "a whole range of food-friendly flavor profiles." Sure to tickle you pink are finds like a dry yet lusty sparkling rosé from biodynamic Austrian producer Meinklang; Roussette de Savoie, an intriguing, refreshing white from eastern France; or even Cabernet Franc from Colorado's own emerging Grand Valley AVA.

Sheer gloss mixed with a little bit of grit—that's the shrewd gist of this downtown arrival.

KALBI SHORTRIBS WITH GREEN PAPAYA SLAW

Says Cummings, "There is something so primitive yet noble about eating with your hands. The vibrant colors and textures of these ribs are not at odds with the gristle and tendon you savagely gnaw—rather, they're in harmony. You show respect to the ingredients when you are willing to get a little dirty with them."

You should be able to find flanken-cut shortribs—three-bone, cross-cut slabs—at your local Asian market, along with many of other listed ingredients (fermented black garlic may also be found at high-end spice shops). The Thai chili sauce—Cummings's version of Sriracha, which, he jokes, "is now so American that you can find it in most Mexican restaurants"—must be made at least a week in advance, though it will keep for several more in the refrigerator, as will the hoisin sauce.

(SERVES 4)

For the Thai chili sauce:

2 pounds Fresno chiles, destemmed and deseeded

3 cloves black garlic

2 cloves roasted garlic (obtained by cutting garlic head in half crosswise, drizzling with olive oil, wrapping in foil, and baking at 350°F for about 25 minutes)

2 cloves fresh garlic

1 teaspoon granulated garlic

2 tablespoons salt

3 tablespoons sugar

1 cup rice wine vinegar

For the spicy hoisin sauce:

½ cup hoisin

3 tablespoons *gochujang* (Korean chili paste)

2 tablespoons *sambal oelek* (Indonesian chili paste)

1 tablespoon rice wine vinegar

1 tablespoon agave nectar

For the green papaya slaw:

2 tablespoons vegetable oil

2 tablespoons soy sauce

1 teaspoon tamarind paste

1 cup julienned green papaya

⅔ cup julienned carrot

½ cup julienned kimchee (fermented, spiced cabbage)

¼ cup julienned cucumber

12 grape tomatoes, halved

18–20 leaves cilantro, minced

6–8 leaves mint, minced

Salt and pepper to taste

4 flanken-cut slabs beef shortribs

Pinches of salt and pepper

1 tablespoon vegetable oil

4 leaves Bibb lettuce

Special equipment:

outdoor grill

To make the Thai chili sauce: Place all ingredients in a food processor and grind just until chunky. Store the mixture in a plastic container, covered with plastic wrap, in your refrigerator for 1 week. When ready to use, return the mixture to the food processor and blend until smooth. Over a medium-hot burner, pass the mixture through a fine-mesh strainer into a medium-size pot and simmer for 5 minutes. Fill a large bowl with ice, transfer the sauce to a heatproof plastic container, and place it in the ice bath to cool.

For the hoisin sauce: Whisk all ingredients together in a mixing bowl until combined. Set aside.

Prepare your outdoor grill.

While it's heating, make the green papaya slaw: In a good-size mixing bowl, whisk the oil, soy sauce, and tamarind paste until well combined. Fold in the remaining slaw ingredients, adjust seasoning to taste, and set aside.

Season shortribs with salt and pepper, then drizzle with vegetable oil. Place on a very hot grill and cook for 3 minutes on each side; when they're nearly done cooking, glaze them with hoisin sauce (you'll need about 2 tablespoons). Remove and slice the slabs between the bones to yield 3 ribs apiece.

To finish, place a lettuce leaf on each of four serving plates for making wraps as desired. Place a mound of slaw next to the lettuce cups. Add the ribs and drizzle them with chili sauce.

Savoy Spinach Salad with Candied Almonds, Tomato Confit & Green Goddess Dressing

The tomato confit should be made at least a day in advance; use the leftovers on bruschetta. The almonds and dressing can also be completed ahead of time if desired; the latter will keep at least five days in the refrigerator.

(SERVES 4)

For the tomato confit:

1 cup grape tomatoes, left whole
2 cloves garlic
1 cup olive oil
1 sprig fresh thyme
Salt and pepper to taste

For the almonds:

4 fluid ounces water
4 ounces (½ cup) sugar
8 ounces raw, shelled almonds
Pinch of salt
Pinch of *shichimi togarashi*

For the dressing:

1 tablespoon olive oil
3 green onions, trimmed
12 chives, trimmed
2 cloves garlic
2 cups sour cream
1 cup buttermilk
1 teaspoon fish sauce
Salt and pepper to taste

2 cups savoy spinach
2 cups arugula
2 cups kale
Grated Parmesan or Asiago cheese, as desired

For the tomato confit: Place all ingredients in a medium saucepan and heat on low for 12 minutes, until the tomato skins are lightly wrinkled. Store in a plastic container in the refrigerator overnight to meld flavors (add extra olive oil to cover if you plan to keep even longer, up to a week).

To candy the almonds: Place water and sugar in a small pot over medium heat for 10 minutes; when the sugar is dissolved, add almonds and cook for 10 minutes. Drain, then toss almonds with salt and *togarashi* and set on a cooling rack for 30 minutes.

Next, prepare the dressing: Place oil in a pan over a medium burner; when hot, sauté green onion, chives, and garlic for 2 minutes. Remove from heat and let cool. Place the mixture in a blender, add the remaining ingredients, and blend until smooth. Adjust seasoning to taste.

Trim and clean the greens thoroughly, then thinly slice into ribbons (this is called *chiffonade*). Place in a mixing bowl, add approximately 2 tablespoons dressing, and toss thoroughly; adjust dressing to taste. Divide evenly among four salad bowls; top each with four or five pieces tomato confit, five or six almonds, and a sprinkling of cheese. Serve and enjoy!

THE SQUEAKY BEAN

1500 WYNKOOP STREET
DENVER, CO 80202
(303) 623-2665
THESQUEAKYBEAN.NET
CHEF/CO-OWNER: MAX MACKISSOCK
CO-OWNER: JOHNNY BALLEN

Don't let the name fool you. . . . actually, come to think of it, go ahead and let it fool you. The discovery that this is no hippy-dippy tofu hut but rather the site of one of Denver's most startlingly original, multilayered, and just plain fun dining experiences will be all the more delicious.

It also makes for quite the happy ending to a classic industry fairy tale. The original Squeaky Bean was a woefully underequipped LoHi hole-in-the-wall that chef-owner Max Mackissock and his GM-partner Johnny Ballen had, like culinary Cinderellas, lovingly transformed into a cult favorite against all odds—only to be forced out in a lease dispute. The homeless but unbowed duo vowed to relocate; as the months passed and anticipation soared, however, questions as to whether they could possibly live up to the hype began to nag.

The fact that they've managed to surpass all expectations means that said happy ending marks in turn the start of a new chapter, the first in a ripping adventure saga. Occupying prime LoDo real estate, the hot spot—while plenty urbane in sage, seafoam, and pebble hues, from the U-shaped bar and booths to the exhibition kitchen—revels

in quirky decorative flourishes that serve as clues to the merriment to come: a vintage Bingo scoreboard here, a framed photo of Farrah Fawcett there, chandeliers made of spoons. The menu, too, is oh-so-slyly evocative: Perusing descriptions like "red *kuri* squash, *vadouvan,* pear, pine syrup, cashew granola, warm milk broth" or "whey-poached lamb sirloin and *lardo, farro,* shelling beans, grapes," you know you're in for something special. But nothing can quite prepare you for its arrival: The doughnuts filled with liver mousse and fig jam they call "foie longjohns," for instance, are magically presented in a leather-paneled mini treasure chest, while "variations of carrot"—roasted, dehydrated, raw—come intricately arranged, sprinkled with citrus-spiked peanuts, in a dish where a scoop of savory Kaffir-lime ice cream swirls into electric-orange *potage de Crécy* poured tableside. Of course, the cocktail program holds its own, as serious craft—house-made syrups, hand-cut ice cubes, and all that jazz—proves a means to joyfully heretical ends, case in point being the rye Manhattan reconfigured as a Jell-O shot.

As Mackissock explains simply, "We like to take flavors that make sense and use different techniques to achieve novelty." In other words, experimental presentation is just the icing on the cake of kitchen fundamentals; thus, though the following recipe as provided requires some specialized equipment, the ingredients could be prepared very simply with perfectly respectable results. Combine some roasted beets, a few wedges of quality Gouda, a handful of toasted walnuts, and a drizzle of basil vinaigrette, and *voilà!*—you're good to go.

Beet Salad with Aerated Gouda, Basil Pudding & Nut Butter

Throughout this book, I have converted grams to ounces or tablespoons and cups where appropriate. In a few cases, however—including this one—a kitchen scale that measures weight in grams is strongly recommended. You will want to begin this recipe several hours in advance.

(SERVES 4)

For the aerated Gouda:

300 grams skim milk

1 gram agar powder (a seaweed-based gelatin substitute)

3 grams salt

4.5 grams silver-strength (160 bloom) sheet gelatin

2 cups cold water

180 grams aged Gouda, grated finely (preferably on a Microplane)

For the nut butter:

3½ ounces raw almonds

2 ounces walnuts

2 ounces pine nuts

1 teaspoon olive oil

Salt to taste

For the basil pudding:

½ cup basil leaves, stems reserved

225 grams whole milk, divided

55 grams heavy whipping cream

Salt to taste

20 grams agar powder

For the beets:

10 baby red beets, trimmed, greens cleaned and reserved

10 baby Chioggia (also known as candy-cane) beets, trimmed, greens cleaned and reserved

3 tablespoons extra-virgin olive oil, divided

Salt to taste

Juice from 1 lemon

4 beet shoots (immature beets 2–4 inches in length; ask for them at your local farmers' market)

Special equipment:

digital scale

whipped-cream dispenser with nitrous-oxide cartridges

2 (1-quart) Mason jars

juicer with solid-plate attachment (optional)

chinois or other fine-mesh strainer

For the aerated Gouda: Combine the milk, agar, and salt in a small pot and let sit for 10 minutes (this is known as "blooming"). Place the pot over high heat, bring to a boil, and cook for 2 minutes, whisking constantly. Meanwhile, bloom gelatin in a bowl filled with about 2 cups cold water for 5 minutes, then drain.

After lowering the heat to medium, add the Gouda to the pot containing the agar mixture and melt completely, about 30 seconds. Remove pot from the stove and add the bloomed gelatin. Transfer to a blender and blend until smooth.

Pour the mixture into your whipped-cream dispenser and double-charge with nitrous oxide per manufacturer's instructions. Let relax for 10 minutes, then shake well and dispense into your Mason jars; seal immediately and set aside for 5 hours before using. (You will have some left over, which will keep for a few days.)

To make the nut butter: Preheat the oven to 350°F. On a sheet pan, toast separately the almonds for 8–10 minutes, the walnuts for 6–8 minutes, and the pine nuts for 4–6 minutes, checking and tossing gently as necessary for even coloration. Cool to room temperature.

Place the walnuts and pine nuts in a food processor and grind as desired (coarsely if you prefer a chunkier butter, finely if you want it smooth). Toss the almonds in the oil and, using a juicer fitted with the solid-plate attachment or a food processor, grind into butter.

Fold the walnut mixture into the almond butter; season to taste with salt and set aside. You will need 1 cup to complete the recipe (there may be some extra).

Next, prepare the basil pudding: Place basil stems in a saucepan with 150 grams milk and bring to a near boil, then turn off the heat and steep 30 minutes.

Place the leaves in a blender with the remaining 75 grams milk as well as cream and puree; strain the mixture into a bowl through a chinois and season with salt.

Remove basil stems from saucepan and discard, whisk agar into pan to incorporate, and bloom for 10 minutes. Place over high heat and boil for 2 minutes, whisking constantly. Add to the leaf-cream mixture and whisk to combine well.

Pour the contents of the bowl into a clean sheet pan and leave to set for 30 minutes; the consistency should be like Jell-O. Cut into small cubes, place in a blender, and blend to obtain a fluid gel; you may need to add a tablespoon of water in the process, but no more. Here, too, you will need about 1 cup to complete the recipe; there may be some extra.

Lastly, prepare the beets: Preheat the oven to 375°F. In a mixing bowl, toss baby beets with 1 tablespoon olive oil and season with salt. Wrap in aluminum foil in 5 sets of 4 and roast for 40 minutes. Cool and carefully peel. Using a mandoline or working carefully with a sharp knife, slice 4 of the beets (2 of each type) horizontally into disks about 1/16-inch thick; leave the others whole.

In a mixing bowl, toss beet greens with lemon juice, remaining 2 tablespoons olive oil, and a pinch of salt.

Place 3 dollops of basil pudding on each of four plates and spread carefully to form stripes. Place 2 whole red and 2 whole Chioggia beets between the stripes and arrange the greens between the beets. Add 1 slice of red beet and 1 slice of Chioggia beet to each plate. Using a spoon, garnish the perimeter of the salad with 2 *quenelles* (oval-shaped dollops) of aerated Gouda and 2 *quenelles* of nut butter. Place 1 beet shoot on top of each salad and serve.

Steuben's

523 East 17th Avenue
Denver, CO 80203
(303) 830-1001
STEUBENS.COM
Owners: Josh and Jenny Wolkon; Chef: Brandon Biederman

It opened only in 2006, but you can't tell by looking that Steuben's hasn't been there, at the edge of Uptown, forever. It's not just the retro design, though certainly the place is steeped in midcentury accents—auto-body hues, swooping lines, shiny vinyl, vintage posters, and all. Nor is it the generous operating hours—though they don't hurt; that welcome mat takes a beating day in and day out. It's not even the fact that the keepers of the bar were slinging Prohibition-era cocktails and revivalist tiki drinks long before anyone else in town—though that, too, is true.

Primarily, of course, it's the comfort food that earns Steuben's its timeless feel. As a coast-to-coast anthology of American classics, the menu invites pretty much everyone, from anywhere, to share in the nostalgia: barbecued ribs, hush puppies, and coconut cake from down South. Chicken Parm and sausage with peppers like you'd find in Little Italy. New England–style lobster rolls, Miami-style *cubanos,* Philly cheesesteaks, Southwestern breakfast burritos with green chile. And so on, and so on: There's nary a spot on the map that some dish or other doesn't point to. Including, perhaps, your childhood home: Think tomato soup and grilled cheese sandwiches, pork chops with green beans, and pie for dessert. But the combination of youthful verve and old soul Steuben's exudes—that's all Denver in a nutshell.

Meatloaf

Chef Brandon Biederman serves this up with good old mashed potatoes and gravy as well as braised collard greens.

(SERVES 4–6)

10 slices bacon, diced

1 white onion, diced

¾ cup diced celery

3 cloves garlic, chopped

2 eggs

1 cup milk

7 slices white bread, cut into small pieces

1½ tablespoons Dijon mustard

2 teaspoons Worcestershire sauce

1 teaspoon Tabasco Sauce

2½ teaspoons salt

½ teaspoon pepper

¾ teaspoon dried basil

½ teaspoon dried thyme

1½ pounds ground beef

1½ pounds ground veal

Butter to coat the pan

½ cup ketchup

3 tablespoons white vinegar

1 tablespoon brown sugar

Special equipment:

11 x 9 x 5-inch loaf pan

Preheat the oven to 350°F.

In a medium pan over low heat, sauté bacon until just crisp, about 5 minutes. Add onion, celery, and garlic and sauté until tender, 7–8 minutes.

In a large bowl, combine eggs, milk, and bread. Mix by hand until the bread is thoroughly incorporated. Add mustard, Worcestershire, Tabasco, salt, pepper, and dried herbs; whisk to combine. Add bacon mixture.

In another large bowl, combine the ground beef and veal. Once integrated, add the ingredients from the first bowl and fully combine.

Grease an 11 x 9 x 5-inch loaf pan with butter. Place the meatloaf in the pan and press down slightly to compact.

In a small bowl, combine the ketchup, vinegar, and sugar well to produce a glaze. Coat the top of the meatloaf with half the glaze, then bake for 45 minutes. Remove from oven, spoon remaining glaze over the meatloaf, return to oven, and bake for an additional 20 minutes. Slice and enjoy!

STREET KITCHEN ASIAN BISTRO

10111 INVERNESS MAIN STREET, SUITE B
ENGLEWOOD, CO 80112
(303) 799-9800
STREETKITCHENASIANBISTRO.COM
CHEF/OWNER: MARY NGUYEN

Bright and airy and flanked by an open kitchen, the dining room of this Englewood outlier bears some resemblance to the bustling markets of Southeast Asia depicted in the full-color photos mounted on its walls, hence the first half of the name. But the sleek furnishings and mod light fixtures lend it a polish worthy of the second half. Having long excelled at the amalgamation of Vietnamese street cuisine and its upscale counterpart at Parallel Seventeen (page 142), chef-owner Mary Nguyen took it a big step further by incorporating Chinese, Japanese, Thai, and Malaysian elements into the mix—and daring to serve it all up in the shadow of the Denver Tech Center as a quirky alternative in a suburb "dominated by big corporate restaurants," in her words.

Combining recipes from her own family—who immigrated to the States after the Vietnam War—with those of the cooks she has met in her travels throughout the region, Nguyen devised a menu that juxtaposes traditional specialties and their contemporary variants at length: dumplings and sushi rolls, rice and noodle bowls, stir-fries and curries. Annotated according to their respective country of origin, they take you on a whirlwind trip from Hong Kong and Hanoi to Bangkok and Penang—some covering more familiar ground than others, as in the case of old-school egg rolls with hot mustard for dipping, crispy *gyoza* (potstickers), *pho bo,* and pad thai. But if you're set on adventure, go for the Japanese scallion pancake (*okonomiyaki*), the Malaysian coconut soup with shrimp and tofu known as *kare laksa,* or the signature roulade of roast pork belly with garlic and chives. Or better still, sign up for one of the five-course theme dinners Nguyen hosts monthly to delve further into any given regional cuisine: a Tour of China, for instance, might kick off with dim sum and rice ale and end with sesame balls and *soju* cocktails.

Nguyen also teaches regularly scheduled cooking classes at the bistro—but you can get a headstart right here.

Blue Crab–and–Goat Cheese Rangoons with Ginger-Pear Dipping Sauce

Nguyen calls this "my rendition of an American Chinese-restaurant classic." The extra sauce, which will keep in the refrigerator for two to three weeks, pairs well with dumplings or duck-based dishes and can even be used as a salad dressing.

(MAKES 20 RANGOONS, SERVING 4–6 AS AN APPETIZER)

For the sauce (yields 3 cups):

1 tablespoon red pepper flakes

2 pieces star anise

1 tablespoon cloves

2 red pears, peeled, cored, and cut into 1-inch cubes

2 ounces brown sugar

4 tablespoons minced ginger

½ tablespoon ground cinnamon

2 cups *mirin* (a sweet rice wine used for cooking, available at Asian groceries)

½ cup sake

¼ cup red wine vinegar

1 ounce (about 2 tablespoons) butter, softened

For the rangoons:

3 quarts canola oil

12 ounces cream cheese, softened

5 ounces goat cheese

½ teaspoon Worcestershire sauce

½ teaspoon light soy sauce

3 tablespoons minced scallion

2 teaspoons minced garlic

1 teaspoon minced ginger

½ teaspoon granulated sugar

½ teaspoon kosher salt

1 dash ground white pepper

1 pound blue crab meat

1 egg

20 square wonton wrappers

Special equipment:

cheesecloth and kitchen string or mesh tea ball

deep-fat fryer and/or frying thermometer

pastry brush

To make the dipping sauce: Place the red pepper flakes, star anise, and cloves at the center of a piece of cheesecloth and tie with string to make a sachet (or place in a tea ball).

In a medium, nonreactive saucepan over medium-high heat, place the sachet with the diced pears, brown sugar, ginger, cinnamon, *mirin,* sake, and vinegar; bring to a boil for 2–3 minutes, then reduce heat to low and cook until pears are tender, about 15 minutes. Remove from heat and let cool, then discard the sachet. Transfer contents to a blender and puree, stopping to add butter a little at a time, until smooth. Set aside.

To make the *rangoons:* Heat oil in a large pot or a deep fryer to 360°F–375°F (check with thermometer).

Make the filling: In a good-size mixing bowl, combine the cheeses well with a wooden spoon. One ingredient at a time, incorporate the Worcestershire sauce, soy sauce, scallion, garlic, ginger, sugar, salt, and pepper. Finally, add the crab and mix to combine, being careful not to break up the clumps too much.

Dampen a clean cloth and set aside. Break the egg into a small glass bowl and whisk lightly to make an egg wash. On a clean, flat surface, lay out a wonton wrapper so that the nearest corner points toward you, forming a diamond shape. With a pastry brush, wet the edges of the wrapper with the egg wash. Add a teaspoon or so of filling to the center and carefully spread it out toward the left and right points of the diamond so that it forms a rectangular shape. Fold the wrapper so that the corner closest to you aligns with the opposite corner, forming a triangle

shape. Seal the edges of the wrapper, adding more egg wash if needed for adhesion. Cover the *rangoon* with the damp cloth and repeat the process with the remaining wrappers and filling, placing each under the cloth as completed.

Carefully add the *rangoons* to the pot or fryer in batches as necessary, taking care not to overcrowd them. Fry until golden, about 3 minutes, turning once. Remove with a slotted spoon and drain on paper towels. Serve immediately with the dipping sauce on the side.

SUSHI TORA

2014 10th Street
Boulder, CO 80302
(303) 444-2280
Owners: Peter and Mara Soutiere; Chef: Ray Srisamer

Upon taking over Sushi Tora, already long established at the west end of Boulder's Pearl Street Mall, in 2008, Peter and Mara Soutiere aimed to "make it different, make it better, make it ours," says Mara. "We're trying to find the new face of sushi."

To that end, they hired Ray Srisamer (pictured)—a Thai-born, Okinawa-trained alum of Austin's acclaimed Uchi—to put his stamp on the standard Japanese repertoire. And so he has. The fundamentals remain: Impeccable seafood is flown in from the world round, and staple sauces like soy and teriyaki are made on-site. The selection of maki and nigiri is light on Americanisms, but not on specialties like *natto* (fermented soybean) and *amaebi* (raw shrimp served with their deep-fried heads), accompanied by premium sake in *masu* (traditional wooden drinking boxes). Yet house originals like the wonderful organic mushroom tempura with green-tea salt, short rib–cabbage wontons, or a composition of *maguro* (yellowfin), Fuji apple, and goat cheese drizzled in pumpkinseed oil subtly shift the parameters of tradition.

As for the setting in which it's all showcased, the Soutieres who also own Tahona Tequila Bistro (1035 Pearl Street, Boulder; 303-938-9600; tahonaboulder.com) around the corner have stuck strikingly, soothingly true to Japanese form. Incorporating pale yellows, glossy blacks, and blond woods, the dining room conveys a serenity broken only by the bustle at the central sushi bar and the drama of a towering flower arrangement or two. It's an invitation to stop, breathe, reflect, and relax—one you'd best not pass up.

HAMA CHILI

A *supreme* is simply the segment of a citrus fruit that's been carefully peeled and segmented with a knife so that only the flesh—no rind or membrane—remains. You should be able to locate fresh mandarins easily during the holiday season; ponzu and orange oil can be found at Asian groceries or even in the Asian section of quality supermarkets.

The yield for this recipe can easily be scaled down or up.

(SERVES 2)

8 mandarin orange *supremes*

8 ounces sushi-grade yellowtail loin, cut into 16 (½-ounce) slices

½–1 bird (Thai) chili, destemmed, deseeded, and sliced thin

1 ounce (2 tablespoons) ponzu sauce

2 teaspoons orange oil

On a serving platter, fan out the orange *supremes* (or divide them evenly between two plates). Lay the sliced yellowtail over the segments, sprinkle it with chilis to taste, and drizzle the ponzu and orange oil over the top.

TAG

1441 LARIMER STREET
DENVER, CO 80202
(303) 996-9985
TAG-RESTAURANT.COM
CHEF/OWNER: TROY GUARD

Stripped down and sexed up, TAG is the red-hot glamour-puss of Larimer Square. High ceilings and low banquettes, origami pendant lamps and lipstick-colored booths, a glass-walled wine tower and a barely there bar define the long, narrow, city-slick space, where LoDo's slinky scenesters fit right in. One night, they're sipping cocktails laced with beet syrup, pumpkin puree, or corn tincture; they're nibbling on East-West inspirations like the signature "sushi tacos" or miso-marinated black cod with edamame salsa and yuzu-spiked eel sauce; they're polishing off such tropically tinged sweets as coconut-chiffon cake with pineapple and mango caramel. And the next day, they're sneaking back on their lunch break, when even the meatloaf is shocked with kimchee and the burger slapped with fried chicken skin. It's all just so exotic.

Yet this isn't chef-owner Troy Guard's only creative outlet. Speaking of burgers, the fall of 2012 saw the launch of TAG Burger Bar in Congress Park (1222 Madison Street,

Denver; 303-736-2260; tagburgerbar.com), where lamb, salmon, excellent veggie patties, and more supplement classic beef, and the toppings range from *chicharrónes* and black bean puree to green papaya slaw and crushed peanuts. Meanwhile, a flight of stairs below TAG itself, TAG | Raw Bar (pictured left; 1423 Larimer Street; 303-996-2685; tagrawbar.com) is the ultimate underground hideaway—part cheerfully glossy, orange-splashed chef's counter and part funky, lo-fi lounge; here, kangaroo *tartare,* buffalo carpaccio accompanied by apples and *li hing* mustard, and scallop rolls garnished with puffed rice and cilantro-lime aioli fill the bill.

In that wild light, the following recipes are surprisingly user friendly—so long, that is, as you're willing to bypass the nearest meat counter in favor of a game specialist like Edwards Meats in Wheat Ridge (12280 West 44th Avenue; 303-422-4397; edwards -meats.com), where you can score both bison and venison loin. (Best to have a kitchen scale on hand for precise measuring as well.)

"Surf-and-Turf" Bison-and-Lobster Sushi

The Japanese mayonnaise brand Kewpie is easily available at Asian markets and even some gourmet retailers, as are sushi rice and *nori* (a type of seaweed). A one-pound lobster will yield approximately double the amount of meat you need for this recipe, which itself can easily be doubled to yield two rolls.

(MAKES ONE 8-PIECE ROLL)

For the lobster mix:

1½ ounces cooked, chopped lobster meat
1 tablespoon Kewpie mayonnaise
1 teaspoon chives
Pinch each of salt and pepper

½ sheet roasted *nori*
2½ ounces sushi rice, measured raw and cooked
    according to package instructions
1 long strip peeled, seeded cucumber, ¼-inch thick
2 strips avocado, ¼-inch thick
1 ounce very thinly sliced raw bison loin
Pinch each of salt and pepper
1 tablespoon Kewpie mayo
1 teaspoon chives

Special equipment:

kitchen scale
sushi rolling mat

To make the lobster mix: Place all ingredients in a bowl; combine well with a spoon and set aside.

Place the *nori* on your rolling mat and spread sushi rice across it, leaving about a ½-inch strip bare. Flip *nori* so that the rice faces down. Place lobster mix in a line across the center of the *nori* sheet, parallel to the bare edge; then top it with strips of cucumber and avocado (they should run the length of the roll). Starting with the bare edge, roll the sheet tightly. Season bison with salt and pepper and lay it atop the roll, then fold the mat around the roll to mold it into shape. Carefully slice sushi into eight pieces and divide the mayonnaise to place a dot atop each piece of bison. Sprinkle with chives and serve.

Venison Tataki with Beets, Arugula Pesto, Aged Gouda & Honey

(SERVES 2 AS AN APPETIZER)

For the beets:

Kosher salt as directed

2 ounces red beet (about 1 small), trimmed

2 ounces golden beet (about 1 small), trimmed

5 teaspoons olive oil, divided

½ teaspoon chives, divided

For the pesto:

2 ounces arugula, cleaned

1 clove garlic, peeled

2 tablespoons white sesame seeds, toasted in
    a dry pan over medium heat until fragrant

½ ounce pecorino, shredded

Pinch each of salt and pepper

2 tablespoons water

¼ cup salad oil

4 ounces venison loin, sliced thin

Pinches of salt and pepper as directed

1 teaspoon canola oil

1 ounce aged Gouda, shaved

2 teaspoons honey

Special equipment:

kitchen scale (optimal)

To prepare the beets: Preheat the oven to 400°F and spread kosher salt on the bottom of a sheet pan. Rub beets with 1 teaspoon oil, prick with a fork, place on pan, and roast until just soft (start checking them after 25 minutes). Let cool, peel, and dice small. In a small bowl, toss diced red beets with 2 teaspoons olive oil and ¼ teaspoon chives; in another small bowl, do the same with the golden beets and remaining oil and chives. Set aside.

To make the pesto: Combine all the ingredients except oil in a food processor. With the motor running, slowly drizzle in oil until the mixture is emulsified.

Season venison with a pinch or two of salt and pepper. In a very hot pan with the canola oil, sear the meat on all sides until rare, about 1 minute. Set aside to cool.

Using a large spoon, place about 1 tablespoon pesto on each of two serving plates (there should be a little left over); with the back of the spoon, make a long stripe. Divide the venison between the plates next to the pesto. Place an even amount of red and golden beets around the venison, sprinkle Gouda over the top, and drizzle with honey.

Tamayo

1400 Larimer Street
Denver, CO 80202
(720) 946-1433
richardsandoval.com
Chef/Owner: Richard Sandoval
Chef de Cuisine: Arnold Rubio

With a few dozen properties to his name—an estimated thirty-five by the time of publication, including Zengo (page 200)—international restaurateur Richard Sandoval does booming business from Orange County to Dubai. But this purveyor of "modern Mexican cuisine," as he calls his signature take on the cookery of his homeland, was one

of the first, opening in 2001 to anchor Larimer Square's transformation into a downtown destination.

In early 2013, the two-story space underwent major renovations; the long, narrow ground-floor dining room now boasts sleek, hacienda-style chic—all dark browns and stucco whites—though the vivid, Picasso-esque mosaic remains, as does LoDo's only rooftop terrace. And the bar program has been pumped up with a transfusion of premium tequilas. Meanwhile, the kitchen, helmed by Arnold Rubio (pictured), hasn't missed a beat amid all the hubbub, maintaining its focus on ultra-stylized *comida*: enchiladas stuffed with crabmeat and spinach and enriched with mascarpone, for instance. Or filet mignon fired up alongside poblano gratin and cactus salad. Or banana empanadas with coconut ice cream. That's all to the good for those of us who need our fix of hibiscus margaritas and shellfish-Gouda *chiles rellenos* on the regular.

Sopa de Elote

ROASTED CORN SOUP WITH HUITLACOCHE DUMPLING

Huitlacoche, also delightfully known as "corn smut," is a plant fungus used by Mexican cooks to add a mushroomy savor to many a dish. It is, believe it or not, delicious and should be available canned at most Latin markets.

There will be some vinaigrette left over; try it on pork chops.

(SERVES 4)

For the huitlacoche *vinaigrette:*

1 tablespoon *huitlacoche*
1 tablespoon sherry vinegar
1 teaspoon honey
¼ teaspoon salt
¼ teaspoon freshly ground pepper
1 cup canola oil

For the soup:

12 ears corn, with husks
4 cups heavy cream
½ teaspoon salt
¼ teaspoon freshly ground pepper

For the dumplings:

4 teaspoons *huitlacoche*
¼ teaspoon salt
⅛ teaspoon freshly ground black pepper
4 wonton wrappers

Special equipment:

outdoor grill (optional)

Prepare the vinaigrette: In a small, nonreactive bowl, mix the *huitlacoche,* vinegar, honey, salt, and pepper to combine; then slowly whisk in the oil. Set aside. (This may be made up to 2 days in advance and stored, tightly covered, in the refrigerator.)

To make the soup: Preheat your grill or broiler. Leaving the husks on, grill or broil the corn 6 inches from the heat source, turning occasionally, about 20 minutes, or until the husks are charred and the kernels within are brown in spots. Remove and let cool.

Bring a good-size pot of water to a boil. While it's heating, strip the husks and silk from the corn. Holding the ears upright, take a sharp knife and cut the kernels carefully off the cobs by slicing downward. Add the kernels to the pot, lower the heat, and simmer until the kernels are very tender, about 10 minutes. Strain.

Working in batches as necessary, puree the corn in a blender or food processor. Using a rubber spatula, force the pureed corn through a medium-hole sieve into a large saucepan. Discard the solids. Add the cream to the saucepan and simmer over low heat for about 10 minutes; the consistency should be relatively thin, not thick like chowder. Season with salt and pepper and keep warm.

While the soup is cooking, prepare the dumplings: In a small bowl, stir the *huitlacoche* with a fork and season with the salt and pepper. Lay a wonton wrapper on a clean, flat work surface. Place 1 teaspoon *huitlacoche* in the center of the wrapper. Rub the edges with a little water and fold it into a triangle shape to enclose the filling; press the edges together to seal. Repeat with the remaining wrappers and filling.

Bring a medium saucepan of water to a gentle boil, then add the dumplings and cook until tender, about a minute. Remove with a slotted spoon.

Place one dumpling each into four large, shallow bowls. Ladle the soup into the bowls. Drizzle the vinaigrette in a decorative pattern over the top and serve immediately.

TRILLIUM

2134 LARIMER STREET
DENVER, CO 80205
(303) 379-9759
TRILLIUMDENVER.COM
CHEF/OWNER: RYAN LEINONEN

"What you see is what you get," says Ryan Leinonen of Trillium's Scandinavian influence. It's true with respect to design; from the sidewalk, you can observe the entire dining room in all its symmetry and almost abstract simplicity—white, blue, and silver squares and cylinders against a field of brick and wood, neatly centered along an axis marked by a series of rectangles: the sleek, stone-lined fireplace at the entrance, an island bar, the open kitchen in back. And it's equally true of the menu, which outlines in sparkling detail its chef-owner's Finnish heritage as well as his Michigan upbringing.

Listening to Leinonen hold forth on his culinary influences is a treat in itself. A natural storyteller, he conjures his immigrant grandmother's kitchen counter, laden with the makings of meat pasties and beet salad; the lakeside mom-and-pop diners of the Lower Peninsula, "smoked whitefish hanging all over the place"; and the Helsinki farmers' market, where "soft-spoken" folks fry up reindeer croquettes on the spot. "Scandinavian herbs and spices are very floral," he'll explain. "There's lot of tarragon, a lot of dill and cardamom" to accent the "nice, simple, hearty" dishes that "warm your soul from the outside in." Still, Leinonen's food does most of his talking for him, bite by bite. At once rootsy and ethereal, earthy and dreamy, it's built on creamy cheeses and dark breads, puddings and pickles, forest flora and freshwater fish in myriad guises. Small plates form a smorgasbord of wonders, from salmon cured in caraway-scented *aquavit* to the extraordinary signature of foie gras mousse served with pickled chanterelles and cranberry coulis over a griddled flatbread called *rieska*. Beautifully composed entrees based on pan-roasted trout, seared duck breast, or grilled pork chops abound in robust accompaniments: sweet-potato spaetzle and caramelly *gjetost* fondue, charred baby onions and plum relish. Desserts arrive redolent of orchard fruits and foraged berries, toasted nuts and candied ginger—and so, too, do cocktails, embellishing the tale of Trillium via mulling spices and feathery herbs.

Take one as a nightcap in the lounge area—where couches strewn with woven pillows surround end tables based on bundled logs—and bask in the Nordic aura. Upon leaving, you'll hardly believe you just sipped *glogg* in the heart of the beer-splashed Ballpark district.

STEELHEAD TROUT RAAKA

Raaka means "raw" in Finnish; as a culinary term, it's the equivalent of French *tartare* and Italian *crudo*.

(SERVES 4)

1 pound steelhead trout fillet, skinned and deboned
    (sockeye or coho salmon may be substituted)
1 small fennel bulb, trimmed and finely diced
1 Fuji apple, skin on, cored and finely diced
1 shallot, finely diced
1 tablespoon olive oil
1 teaspoon fresh grated horseradish
1 teaspoon kosher salt
Zest of 1 lemon
4 slices marbled rye bread, toasted and sliced
    diagonally
Whitefish roe as desired

With a very sharp knife, cut the trout fillet lengthwise into thin strips, then dice the strips as finely as possible. Place in a bowl in the refrigerator.

In a good-size mixing bowl, combine well all remaining ingredients except bread and roe. Add the fish and combine thoroughly. Taste and adjust seasoning as necessary.

Top each slice of rye toast with a small dollop of whitefish roe; place two slices on each of four plates. Add *raaka* in evenly divided mounds and serve immediately.

LEMON-AND-DILL PICKLED SHRIMP

Prepare this recipe a day in advance; it's perfect for a small dinner party.

(SERVES 10 AS AN APPETIZER)

5 pounds (16/20-count) raw shrimp, peeled,
    tails on, and deveined
6 shallots, julienned
6 garlic cloves, thinly sliced
1 bunch fresh dill, roughly chopped
1 teaspoon celery salt
1 teaspoon fennel seeds
1 teaspoon mustard seeds
1 teaspoon ground coriander
1 teaspoon kosher salt
Zest and juice of 4 lemons
¼ cup Champagne vinegar
2 tablespoons extra-virgin olive oil

In a large bowl, prepare an ice bath. In a large pot, bring 3 gallons water to a boil over high heat. Add shrimp and immediately turn off the heat. Allow to poach until almost cooked—they should be flexible but no longer transparent. Immediately drain the shrimp and shock in the ice bath.

Combine all remaining ingredients in a large bowl; when the shrimp have cooled, drain and add them to the bowl and toss gently to combine thoroughly. Place in an airtight container and refrigerate for at least 12 hours. Serve arranged on a platter or in a large bowl alongside a smaller bowl for discarding the tails.

TWELVE RESTAURANT

2233 Larimer Street
Denver, CO 80205
(303) 293-0287
TWELVERESTAURANT.COM
Chef/Owner: Jeff Osaka

With its wood-planked floors worn to a sheen, clean lines, subdued hues, and warm lighting, the dining room of Jeff Osaka's contemporary American sleeper comes about as close to the one in your dream home as possible. Yet, the Los Angeles transplant admits, "twelve actually didn't start as I imagined." Opening in the gritty Ballpark neighborhood just as the first signs of gentrification were beginning to show back in

2008, "I looked around and realized how crazy I was to try to serve up thirty-five-dollar entrees when my customers had to step over a couple of people just to get through the door. I lowered prices, but to this day, people still think we're the 'expensive' restaurant," he laughs.

He can afford to be amused; after all, he's developed a following of hardcore regulars (among them many a colleague) who know the food is worth every penny. As the name suggests, twelve's entire selection changes monthly—"and after forty-eight menus, I think we are still evolving." Such understatement is typical of this soft-spoken master of precise technique. His way with foie gras and duck bids you stop to marvel mid-bite; his vegetarian creations are remarkably complex yet sensuous, as with brie-enriched mushroom Wellington alongside garlic spinach and parsnip puree. Desserts always incorporate seasonal fruits in thoughtful fashion, and the wine list is updated accordingly. In the midst of a full-scale neighborhood transformation—whose growth, Osaka observes, "doesn't appear to be stopping anytime soon!"—this cozy little hideaway has all the makings of a permanent destination.

CHILLED MELON SOUP WITH FRESH RICOTTA, PROSCIUTTO & BASIL

(SERVES 4)

1 large or 2 small Rocky Ford (or other) cantaloupe
1 cup apple juice
1 tablespoon lime juice
¼ teaspoon salt
2–3 tablespoons sugar as needed
Ice water as needed
¼ cup fresh ricotta
2 slices prosciutto *crudo,* diced into ¼-inch pieces
1 basil leaf, cut in *chiffonade*
1 tablespoon extra-virgin olive oil, preferably Ligurian

Place the melon(s) on a flat surface and cut in half. Use a spoon to scoop out and discard the seeds; scoop out the flesh into a large, nonreactive bowl. Yield should be about 3 tightly packed cups cantaloupe.

Place melon in blender; add apple juice, lime juice, and salt and puree until smooth. Taste and adjust seasoning. Add sugar if needed; you may also add ice water to adjust consistency—the soup should not be too thick or too thin. Return to bowl and refrigerate an hour or more to chill until ready to serve.

In the center of each of four serving bowls, place a dollop of ricotta and top with an evenly divided amount of diced prosciutto, basil, and drizzled olive oil. Put chilled soup into a pitcher and pour tableside. Enjoy!

"Chicken Fried" Ris de Veau with Country Gravy, Potato Puree & Poppy Seed Slaw

You'll need most of a day to complete this recipe, but it's sure to wow dinner guests. Any reputable butcher should be able to take an advance order for sweetbreads.

(SERVES 4)

For the sweetbreads & gravy:

1–1½ pounds veal sweetbreads
1 large carrot, peeled and diced small
1 large and 1 medium onion, separately diced small
1 rib celery, washed and diced small
1 bay leaf
½ cup dry white wine
2 quarts water
1 cup buttermilk
1 tablespoon butter
1 slice bacon, diced
1 sprig thyme
1 teaspoon plus 2 cups all-purpose flour
2 cups heavy cream
Oil for deep-frying, such as peanut, safflower, or canola,
    as directed
1 tablespoon each salt and freshly ground black pepper
Pinch of cayenne pepper

For the potato puree:

1 cup heavy cream
3 large russet potatoes, cut into 1-inch dice
Salt and freshly ground black pepper as directed
4 tablespoons unsalted butter, softened
2 tablespoons sour cream

For the poppy seed slaw:

⅓ cup sugar
½ cup apple cider vinegar
1 teaspoon salt
1 teaspoon ground dry mustard
1 cup canola oil

3 tablespoons poppy seeds, toasted lightly in a dry pan
3 cups thinly shaved green cabbage
1 cup thinly shaved red cabbage
1 medium carrot, grated
1 small red onion, shaved thin
2 scallions, sliced thin on bias

Special equipment:

deep-frying thermometer
potato ricer

In a large bowl filled with ice water, soak sweetbreads in the refrigerator for at least 8 hours, changing water two or three times. Drain and set aside.

Add carrot, diced large onion, celery, and bay leaf together with white wine and 2 quarts of water to a heavy 4-quart saucepan. Bring to a boil over medium-high heat; meanwhile, prepare an ice bath. Gently add sweetbreads to the pan and wait for the liquid to return to a boil; then reduce heat to a simmer and cook until sweetbreads are plump and slightly firm to the touch, about 3 minutes.

With a slotted spoon, place sweetbreads in the ice bath to stop the cooking. Once they're chilled, transfer them to a surface covered with paper towels or a cloth napkin and pat dry. Cut away any fat or connective tissue with a small paring knife, reserving the scraps. Pull apart the sweetbread lobes (they will separate naturally) into bite-size pieces. Place them in a bowl, add buttermilk, and allow to soak in refrigerator for at least 1 hour.

Meanwhile, place the butter, bacon, thyme, remaining diced onion, and reserved sweetbread scraps in a medium saucepan over medium heat. Cook a few minutes, until onions and fat begin to brown; add 1 teaspoon flour and use a wooden spoon to scrape browned bits off bottom of pan (this is where all the flavor is). Add cream, stirring frequently to avoid scorching, and reduce by half, until the mixture has a medium-thick consistency. Season to taste and keep warm.

While the gravy is reducing, begin the potatoes: Warm the cream in a small saucepan over medium heat and set aside. Place potatoes in a medium saucepan with cold water to cover and bring to a boil. Add 1 tablespoon salt, reduce heat to a simmer, and cook for about 15–20 minutes, or until tender; keep warm.

Next, make the slaw. Combine the sugar, vinegar, salt, and mustard in a large stainless-steel bowl. Whisk in canola oil, add poppy seeds, and transfer to a jar with a tight-fitting lid. Using the same bowl, combine the remaining slaw ingredients; shake the dressing jar well, add desired amount to the slaw (there will likely be some left over), and toss to coat. Set aside.

To fry the sweetbreads, add oil to a high-sided pan to reach 4 inches in depth and bring to 350°F over high heat (check with thermometer).

In a medium bowl, place remaining 2 cups flour with salt, pepper, and cayenne and stir to combine. Using a slotted spoon, remove sweetbread pieces from buttermilk and transfer to seasoned flour. Coat completely, dusting off the excess flour, and carefully drop into the hot oil (it could splatter). Fry for about 2 minutes or until crispy, then transfer to a plate lined with paper towels.

Pass the potatoes through a ricer or food mill into a large mixing bowl. Whisk in warm cream, softened butter, and sour cream, then season with salt and pepper to taste.

Spoon a dollop of potato puree on each of four plates. Use spoon to create a well in the potatoes; ladle country gravy into the wells. Place an even amount of sweetbreads next to the potatoes, add a scoop of slaw, and enjoy!

Vesta Dipping Grill

1822 Blake Street
Denver, CO 80202
(303) 296-1970
vestagrill.com
Owners: Josh and Jenny Wolkon; Chef: Brandon Foster

In myriad comforting ways, Vesta Dipping Grill hasn't changed a bit since it opened in 1997; in as many exciting ways, it just keeps getting better. "After fifteen years, there's an interesting line to walk in terms of remaining true to who you've been, so the people who supported you all that time get what they want, and at the same time trying to stay current," muses Josh Wolkon, who also owns Steuben's (page 173) and Ace Eat Serve (page 1). He should know—between the departure of longtime chef Matt Selby (who provided the recipe that follows) and a series of planned renovations to the space, he's got his hands full.

Housed in what was, more than a century ago, a spice factory, the capacious dining room still feels like the place to be it is: High ceilings, wood floors, a long concrete bar, circular booths the size of hot tubs, and sculptural copper and steel positively vibrate with

energy—and as Wolkon puts it, "you don't want to turn a warm red glow bright blue." In short, the updates won't be drastic—some reupholstering here, some polishing there— except up front, where Vesta's facade will eventually open up to the street.

As for the menu, it was always built to last, revolving as it does around everybody's favorite food group: dipping sauce. Which isn't to say it hasn't evolved as it revolves— the original emphasis on skewers has long since been replaced by a combination of small and large plates that, to quote Wolkon, "stand on their own" but are nonetheless designed to complement an array of mix-and-match condiments: think pineapple marmalade, wasabi syrup, and black pepper aioli alongside *kabocha* squash tamales, venison sausage, or southern Indian chickpea crepes. (The rather underrated bar program is no less vital, from the extensive and gutsy wine list to the barrel-aged cocktails.)

Now, Selby's successor (Brandon Foster, pictured) "deserves the opportunity to put his stamp on the kitchen—but at the end of the day, you try to make your guests happy," says Wolkon. It's a mature outlook to underscore the fact that "Vesta has grown up just as we have."

CHILI-ORANGE RIB TIPS WITH THAI BASIL– BUTTERMILK DIP & CORIANDER SUGAR

This appetizer requires some advance preparation, as the riblets should be marinated overnight. An Asian grocery should carry many of the following ingredients.

(SERVES 4)

For the rib tips:

Zest and juice of 3 oranges

1 cup bottled orange juice

½ cup tamarind juice

2 tablespoons yellow curry paste

4 Kaffir lime leaves, chopped

¼ cup brown sugar

3 pounds pork riblets

Salt and pepper to rub

2 bird (Thai) chilies, minced

1 tablespoon scallions, sliced thin

For the dip:

½ cup Thai basil, packed

1 cup buttermilk

½ cup plain yogurt

2 tablespoons corn syrup

2 teaspoons salt

For the coriander sugar:

2 tablespoons coriander seed

1 cup sugar

2 tablespoons salt

Special equipment:

spice grinder or coffee mill

In a mixing bowl, combine the orange zest and fresh juice with the bottled orange juice, tamarind juice, curry paste, lime leaves, and brown sugar. Whisk to combine.

Generously season riblets on all sides with salt and pepper. Place in a baking dish large enough to accommodate both the riblets and the marinade. Pour marinade over the ribs and toss carefully to coat; cover with foil and marinate in the refrigerator overnight.

Preheat the oven to 250°F. Place the covered dish in the oven and braise for 2½ hours. Remove the riblets, discard the braising liquid, and then return the riblets to the dish; let cool, covered, in the refrigerator.

Meanwhile, make the dip: Place a small pot of salted water over high heat and bring to a boil. Blanch the basil leaves in the boiling water for about 30 seconds; remove with a slotted spoon and rinse under cold water. Wring out excess moisture and place in a blender with the buttermilk, yogurt, corn syrup, and salt. Puree until smooth.

To make the coriander sugar, toast the coriander seeds until fragrant in a small sauté pan, about a minute. Grind the toasted seeds in a spice grinder, then place in a small bowl with the sugar and salt. Use a whisk to combine thoroughly.

Preheat the oven to 500°F.

Once the riblets are chilled, cut them between the bones to make bite-size, bone-in pieces. Place rib tips on a baking sheet and reheat for 8–10 minutes. Remove from oven and toss with the chilies and scallions.

Equally distribute the tips among four plates and serve with dishes of buttermilk dip and coriander sugar for dipping and sprinkling.

ZENGO

1610 Little Raven Street
Denver, CO 80202
(720) 904-0965
richardsandoval.com
Chef/Owner: Richard Sandoval
Chef de Cuisine: Clint Wangsnes

In 2004, the Denver dining scene was just beginning to emerge from its cocoon of so-called cowtown cuisine; already blinking in the light of such dazzling destinations as Jennifer Jasinski and Beth Gruitch's Bistro Vendôme (page 18), Frank Bonanno's Mizuna, and Restaurant Kevin Taylor, many a fledging local foodie had yet to see anything quite like the spicy, sexy new sanctuary of Asian-Latin fusion called Zengo.

We've come a long, long way since—indeed, by all accounts of recent national press, we've arrived. And yet there's still no place in town quite like jet-setting chef-restaurateur Richard Sandoval's Riverfront Park go-to. It's not that other chefs haven't taken to blending Eastern and Western traditions with aplomb; they have. Nor is it that the decor—for all its sensuous lines and lipstick gloss—is unmatched in its flirty urbanity;

it isn't. But perhaps it's fair to say that few others have so consistently highlighted the binary glamour of fusion—be it the bar's equal emphasis on tequila and sake or the juxtaposition of sesame and chipotle, tempura and tortillas, *huitlacoche* and dragon sauces executed by chef de cuisine Clint Wangsnes (pictured).

Which isn't to imply Zengo never changes. With more than thirty restaurants spanning the globe from Las Vegas to Qatar, the Mexico City–bred Sandoval nevertheless finds time to oversee the implementation of new ideas not only here but also at his downtown Denver flagship, Tamayo (page 186), and at tapas bar Al Lado, right next door to Zengo (as its Spanish name suggests; 303-572-3000). Take "Test Kitchen," a selection of seasonally changing menu items inspired by the combination of two specific traditions: the Philippines and Argentina, for instance, or Mexico and Korea (the latter yielding the likes of seafood-scallion pancakes with avocado-corn salad and adobo-roasted chicken with chorizo and kimchee). Or take the long-awaited arrival of weekend brunch service, featuring all-you-can-eat, prix-fixe small plates such as Peking duck *chilaquiles* and bacon-and-egg steamed buns (*bao*) with salsa verde.

In short, Zengo just keeps going, and we keep coming.

Thai Chicken Empanadas

Reserve about three hours to complete this recipe (longer if you don't already have any grilled chicken on hand). You should be able to find Oaxaca cheese—a Mexican cow's milk cheese similar to mozzarella in texture—at Latin markets.

(MAKES ABOUT 30 EMPANADAS)

1 poblano chile
2 teaspoons olive oil, divided
Salt and pepper as directed
1 cup small-dice onions
1 pound grilled chicken breast, diced
½ bunch cilantro, minced
Generous ⅓ cup Thai sweet chili sauce
6 ounces Oaxaca cheese, shredded (or substitute with mozzarella)
All-purpose flour for dusting
2 pounds (4 sheets) puff pastry, refrigerated
6 cups canola oil

Special equipment:
3½-inch biscuit cutter
frying thermometer

Preheat the oven to 400°F.

Rub poblano with 1 teaspoon olive oil and season with a pinch each salt and pepper. Wrap in foil and roast until softened, about 30 minutes (check after 20 minutes for doneness). Remove from the oven and set aside until cool enough to handle, then peel, deseed, and dice small.

Heat a large sauté pan over medium-high heat. Add remaining teaspoon olive oil and sauté the onions about 8 minutes or until translucent, stirring frequently. Remove from heat.

In a large bowl, toss to combine the poblanos, onions, chicken, 1½ teaspoons salt, 1 teaspoon pepper, cilantro, chili sauce, and cheese. Taste and adjust seasoning as necessary. You should have an ample 3 cups filling; cover and refrigerate until chilled, at least 1 hour (can be stored overnight).

On a lightly floured board, roll out one sheet of puff pastry, leaving the others in the refrigerator until ready to use. Using a biscuit cutter, cut out rounds of dough. Retrieve the filling from the refrigerator and place about 1½ tablespoons in the center of one round. To fold the empanada, hold the round in one hand so it forms a U shape; with the fingers of your other hand, press the filling down. (It may initially seem as though there is too much filling, but as you press on it, the dough will stretch.) Seal the package completely by first pressing the edges firmly with your fingers, then using a fork to crimp them. Refrigerate and continue with the remaining rounds, then repeat the entire process with the remaining sheets of puff pastry to yield roughly 30 empanadas (give or take a few).

In a large, heavy-bottomed pot, heat the canola oil over high heat to 350°F. Fry the empanadas a few at a time until golden brown, about 3 minutes each. Drain on a rack or a baking sheet lined with paper towels. Once drained, serve immediately.

Glossary

What's basic vocabulary to one cook is foreign language to another. Although a glossary comprehensive enough to serve the needs of novices and avid kitcheneers alike would fill its own book, the following may shed some added light on recipe notations.

Bird chilies: These small, thin cultivars may also be called "bird's eye chilies" or "Thai chilies."

Black garlic: When garlic is fermented, it becomes dark, soft, and sweet. Once hard to find, it's now available at some specialty spice shops.

Blooming: An important step in recipes that contain gelatin, which must be soaked (hence softened) prior to cooking.

Chiffonade: The technique to create a chiffonade involves slicing stacked, rolled leaves of greens or herbs into long, thin strips.

Chile/chili: We have taken to spelling the name of one of the world's most popular flavoring agents with an *e* in Latin contexts and an *i* in Asian contexts.

Chinois/China cap: Generally interchangeable terms for a fine-meshed, conical strainer, used to produce smooth sauces and soups.

Deglazing: This technique involves adding liquid to a pan in which food has just been cooked to loosen the sticky bits and, often, to provide the foundation for a sauce.

Double straining: Cocktails that are double-strained are poured from a shaker, which has its own strainer, through a fine-mesh sieve to remove solids.

Gochujang: Fermented Korean chili-and-soy paste.

Huitlacoche: This cornstalk fungus is considered a delicacy in Mexico—hence the nickname "Mexican truffle." Intensely earthy in character, it may be found canned in Latin markets. Also known as "corn smut."

Julienne: Julienned ingredients are cut into thin, matchstick-like pieces.

Ketjap manis: Also *kecap manis,* this is a thick, sweet, gently spiced Indonesian soy sauce.

Kimchee: The national side dish/condiment of Korea contains cabbage fermented with chili, garlic, and fish or shrimp sauce.

Mandoline: An adjustable plane slicer designed to ensure uniform thinness.

Muddling: Mixologist's term for mashing solid ingredients. Though the back of a spoon will often suffice, a wooden muddling stick is preferable, as it won't scratch glass.

Nonreactive cookware: Stainless-steel and ceramic pots and pans (along with glass and plastic storage containers) are preferred over their copper, cast-iron, and aluminum equivalents for recipes that contain highly acidic ingredients such as tomatoes, vinegar, or citrus, which can react with certain metals.

Panko: Japanese bread crumbs, valued for their light, crispy texture.

Piment d'espelette: Espelette pepper, to use the English translation, is a type of paprika from France. The brick-red spice should be available from most gourmet retailers.

Ponzu: Soy sauce, rice wine and vinegar, seaweed, and citrus juice—namely that of the mandarin orange–like yuzu—are the traditional ingredients of this Japanese condiment. You can purchase bottled versions or make your own, much as you would a vinaigrette.

Preserved lemon: Brightly flavored salt-pickled lemons are most commonly associated with North African cuisine.

Quenelle: In classical contexts, a quenelle is a savory poached dumpling. In modern usage, the word refers to any item that possesses the oval shape of its original referent; ice cream, mashed potatoes, preserves, and other soft foods can be molded into quenelles between two spoons.

Roll cut: Cylindrical vegetables, such as carrots or zucchini, chopped on a bias are roll cut. Hold your knife at a 45-degree angle and make a diagonal slice, then rotate the vegetable up to a half turn and repeat.

Sambal oelek: Indonesian chili paste.

Shichimi togarashi: Also known as "seven-spice powder," this Japanese spice mixture typically contains Sichuan peppercorns, chilies, dried orange or tangerine peel, sesame seeds, and seaweed flakes as well as garlic, ginger, and/or poppy seeds.

Simple syrup: Equal parts sugar and water, boiled until the former has dissolved completely. Though you can buy bottled versions, it's very easy (simple, in fact) to make yourself.

Speck: This traditional ham hails from the Italian-Austrian border region known both as Alto Adige and the Südtirol; accordingly, it splits the difference between prosciutto and Black Forest ham, being more pungent than the former yet gentler than the latter.

Sweat: When you sweat ingredients, you are simply cooking them over relatively gentle heat so that they soften but don't brown.

Tamari: A type of *shoyu* (Japanese soy sauce) made with less (or no) wheat, prized for its relative viscosity.

Twist: The classic cocktail garnish is most simply made by peeling a long, narrow strip of zest from a citrus fruit, avoiding the pith as much as possible and trimming the edges as necessary, then wrapping it around a thin, cylindrical implement (such as a skewer).

Index

About the Author

Ruth Tobias is a longtime food-and-beverage writer, assistant editor at *Sommelier Journal,* and author of the blog *Denveater.* She is also the author of *Food Lovers' Guide to Denver & Boulder* (Globe Pequot Press).

Kansas-born and Oklahoma-bred, Tobias received her BA in English from, the University of California at Los Angeles in 1992 and her MFA in poetry from the University of Iowa Writers' Workshop in 1995. In 1997, she moved east to study literature as a PhD candidate at Boston University; it was there that her fascination with all things edible and potable began to alter her career plans, and since the turn of the millennium she has been publishing her work in regional and national publications, completing certificate programs along the way at The Cambridge School of Culinary Arts and the International Wine Guild in Denver—where she now lives with her partner Brit and cats Jasper and Myshkin.

About the Photographer

Christopher Cina, a chef by trade, picked up photography late in life while publishing his recipes on his food blog. Soon after it became an obsession and five years later has morphed into a second career. While Christopher still shoots in his home kitchen, he also does photography work for several Denver area restaurants and local charity events. When he is not in the kitchen, Christopher can be found doting on his three daughters. He is available online at christophercina.com.